A Far Green Country

Hiking Tips from Isle Royale National Park

Greg M. Romaneck

**Illustrations & Art Design
By
Kyle M. Romaneck**

"A Far Green Country: Hiking Tips from Isle Royale National Park," by Greg M. Romaneck. ISBN 978-1-60264-402-1.

Published 2009 by Virtualbookworm.com Publishing Inc., P.O. Box 9949, College Station, TX 77842, US. ©2009, Greg M. Romaneck. All rights reserved.

Manufactured in the United States of America.

Introduction

Every journey has its own flavor. When a person travels it is often in search of things. Perhaps it is the act of seeing new places, people, or terrain. In other instances the impetus to set out on new or familiar trails stems from a need to escape. For some people, travel is a means of reconnecting with their natural roots in a world that can spin all too quickly.

Whatever the reason, our journeys are personally important enough to act as motivational tools that cause us to spring into action. In search of something we sort out our gear, stuff our packs, and ready ourselves for the trip. Hopefully, through careful preparation & focus we are ready to gain from the places we seek out.

One of the more pristine and isolated locations in the lower forty-eight states that beckons to travelers is Isle Royale National Park. Located in the heart of Lake Superior, Isle Royale is an archipelago of over two hundred islands. The main island stretches to a length of nearly fifty miles. Its width varies from one to about nine miles. Within these confines travelers can find a wilderness unlike virtually any other place in the United States.

Isle Royale contains about 165 miles of maintained and interconnected hiking trails. These pathways vary in difficulty from relatively tame to vibrantly difficult. A backpacker interested in doing so can easily plan a hike 3-15 days without really retracing their steps. Isle Royale is a remote place where over 98% of the land remains undeveloped wilderness. A series of campgrounds are maintained across the island and these serve the vast majority of hikers who traverse this wilderness park. Backcountry permits can be secured for off-trail hiking and camping but only a small minority of park visitors uses this privilege.

Located in the northern reaches of one of the world's largest fresh water lakes, Isle Royale can be reached in two ways. A seaplane shuttle can be chartered from the Houghton/Hancock area in Michigan's Upper Peninsula (UP). The flight takes about thirty minutes and costs approximately $240 round trip. A second and more commonly chosen means of arrival is via one of the four ferryboats that head out to the park.

The National Park Service (NPS) operates the *Ranger III* from its dock in Houghton. The *Ranger III* is the largest of the ferryboats operating between the mainland and the park. It makes two weekly passages to Isle Royale's Rock Harbor with the trip taking about seven hours. On board passengers are afforded some musical entertainment as well as occasional lectures conducted by veteran visitors or researchers who are traveling out to the park for study purposes. Travelers can also register and receive their camping permit and observe the required ranger led "Leave No Trace" presentation while en route, thus avoiding the need to do so once they land.

The *Isle Royale Queen IV* makes essentially daily trips to Isle Royale from its home base in Copper Harbor, Michigan. The *Queen* is a dependable ship that takes slightly more than three hours to make its way to or from the park dock at Rock Harbor.

A family-run business, the *Queen* tends to roll a bit more than the other boats but can be counted upon to head out on the date and time it is scheduled to do so. Also, the frequency that the *Queen* travels to Rock Harbor makes it a good choice for a more simplified plan of arrival.

Grand Portage, Minnesota, way up on the Canadian border, is the home to the remaining two ferryboats. The *Wenonah* is a veteran boat that incorporates a bit of sightseeing with the island passage. During its basically daily three-hour passage to Isle Royale, *Wenonah* passengers are given an opportunity to see the wreck of the steamer *America*, Rock of Ages Lighthouse, and the Witches Tree; a noted spiritual place of the Chippewa. The Wenonah is also a family-run business with a long heritage of making this journey between Grand Portage and the park's western terminus, Windigo.

The final ferryboat is the *Voyageur II* also out of Grand Portage. The *Voyageur* is a moderately sized but swift boat that circumnavigates the island on an essentially every other day and clockwise basis. The *Voyageur II* stops at Windigo but heads on along the island's northern shore to overnight at Rock Harbor. Then, on the following day, the boat heads down along the southern shore, back to Windigo, and then out to Grand Portage. There are also several other stops that passengers can charter along both shores of the island. The *Voyageur II* is also a US mail carrier and can be used as both a shuttle around the park and a source of resupply boxes mailed to visitors themselves.

In reflecting on these varied transportation options two things will quickly become clear to a potential Isle Royale visitor. First, it takes careful planning to arrange a trip to this isolated park. Isle Royale is a remote place and the boats & plane that can be used to access it have idiosyncratic schedules. This fact makes itinerary development complex but also exciting. Second, if you want to go to Isle Royale you will have to make some effort. However, with careful planning and some energy, you can have a wonderful time both preparing for and actually visiting this distant place.

This particular book is designed to enhance your next (or first) visit to Isle Royale. The structure of the book is essentially a set of interconnected trail journals that capture separate long hikes in this park. At the close of each daily entry are sequentially numbered hiking tips and suggestions designed to improve your backpacking experience in this park. These tips take many forms and may relate to equipment, conditioning, wildlife observation, terrain, self-improvement, and reflection. Additionally, a few sketches have also been incorporated to offer a visual impression of this beautiful place.

On a personal level, having visited Isle Royale twelve times, it has been this writer's privilege to hike virtually all of the park's trails. In a place where loons call across Northwoods lakes, wolves howl in the night, and moose raise & protect their young it is easy to lose oneself in the wilderness beauty. But even though Isle Royale is a meaningful place to be treasured, it is also a wilderness area that must be treated with respect. Heading out to a place like Isle Royale without thoughtful preparation is not only unwise—it is dangerous.

With this cautionary note in mind, it is hoped that the text which follows will offer insights not only into traveling in Isle Royale but also other wilderness locations you may choose to visit. Some people believe that the entire world is there simply for human development and exploitation. Others think of themselves as separate from nature or as mere observers. In reality we are but parts of a natural order that encompasses & connects all elements of our world. If we can find ourselves and truly connect with wild places, we do more than just recreate. Indeed, it is this act of seeing life's connections through participating in a positive wilderness experience that we shape ourselves and those we come in contact with. Isle Royale is a place where such contact is possible. Hopefully, you will arrive there some day and

find not only the park's natural wonders but yourself as
well.

Dedication

This book is dedicated to my late father whose love of nature has helped shape my outlook on wild things. I owe my father a great deal and mere words cannot communicate my gratitude. Thank you dad and I hope there are lakes, rivers, fields, and mountains for you to see wherever your spirit is.

Acknowledgement: The wolf drawing that introduces section three of this book has been derived from a photograph by a young man from New York State named Dylan Blair. I would like to thank Dylan for sharing his photo of a wolf we both saw near Tobin Harbor, as it was both inspiring and representative of the wild place that Isle Royale remains.

"What business have I in the woods if I am thinking of something out of the woods?"

- Thoreau -

Table of Contents

Part I: Solo Hiking the Greenstone
Ridge 1
Part II: Hiking the West End With
Family 77
Part III: Fall Tips for the End of the
Season 147
Hiking Tips Index 162
Resource Guide 169

"For every walk is a sort of crusade."
- Thoreau -

Part I: Solo Hiking the Greenstone Ridge

"Wildness is the preservation of the world."

- Thoreau -

Day 1 (Friday—June 17): First days on many hiking trips represent a fresh start. Plans made over many months come to fruition after great anticipation. Each start to a new hike offers a unique opportunity to see things never before seen, revisit favorite places, and learn more about yourself & the world around you.

This return visit to Isle Royale was my ninth trip to the park. Therefore, in a very real sense, this hike was a repeat performance. Each of the trails and camps I was scheduled to visit were ones I had seen before. The time of year scheduled for this visit, June, was the month I typically headed north to cross over to the park. My gear was generally the same kit I commonly used. Yet, in a fundamental way, this trip had one central and unique element contained within it. I would be solo hiking across the island & back to my starting point at Rock Harbor. This would mark the first time I had solo hiked on Isle Royale and I looked forward to that experience with great anticipation.

Solo hiking is not something unfamiliar to me. Yet, I had never hiked alone in this remote park. In this light my preparation, both material and psychological, was markedly different than in previous years. When one hikes alone there are questions to address that tandem or group hiking negate:

- How light can I get my pack while still being practical about carrying everything?
- How will I handle carrying shelter, cooking gear, my water filter, and all the other impedimenta usually shared?
- How much more careful should I be as I am alone & help is far away?
- Is hiking as worthwhile with no partner to share with?
- Will I miss speaking with others & having the communion of the trail?

With these and other related thoughts in mind I set out to test myself and rekindle alone the love I have for this park. I hoped for a successful journey and looked forward to sharing highlights with my family and friends once I returned. But there were also some lingering doubts that nipped away at my psychological heels.

At the start of this hike I was concerned about a few personal matters. I had been hospitalized shortly before my scheduled arrival in the park. That brief hospitalization, a negative angiogram, and follow-up medical treatments had taxed me. My normal conditioning regimen prior to hiking season had been broken. When the time came to head north I was in reasonable condition but not quite where I wanted to be. Further, nagging depression linked to my illness, and ongoing & thoughtless work stress had reduced my mental preparation as well. All in all, I arrived in Houghton anxious to get back to a place of peace but also concerned about elements of my usually strong durability.

After spending a moderately restless night sleeping in my van I arrived at the NPS dock just as it opened. There sat the *Ranger III*, gleaming in the morning sunlight. Its blue and yellow colors sparkled and welcomed me. It felt good to look at this familiar vessel. Many of the memories it had transported me to came flooding back into my mind.

The day was absolutely beautiful. The sun shone and a refreshing north wind cooled the air around me. After purchasing a fifty-dollar season pass at the park visitor center located at the dock I checked in my pack and trekking poles for storage on the boat. Then I started to peruse the books for sale in the visitor center. As I was looking at books on wolves & moose I heard a voice behind me say, "I can't believe it. What are the odds of this?"

I turned and saw Bill Manderfield, a local businessman who works on various construction projects inclusive of tasks on the island. I first met Bill and his wife, Maddie, on Isle Royale two years previous to this visit. On that occasion, my eldest son, Kyle, and I spent hours talking with the Manderfields on the boat ride back to Houghton. Subsequently, my family visited the Manderfields in their lovely home in a small town near Houghton. In June of 2004 Kyle and I ran into Bill at the *Ranger III* dock as we headed out to the island on the first boat trip offered that June. The coincidence of once again running into a familiar face after a whole year was stunning.

I sat with Bill during the long ride out to Isle Royale. We parted ways when the boat stopped at park headquarters on Mott Island. Bill was planning to be there for ten days as his company was working on an electrical and plumbing project commissioned by the park service. We wished each other well and headed in different directions. Life is strange sometimes & I do not think everything is merely random or coincidental.

After docking at Rock Harbor I swiftly picked up my gear, grabbed my two trekking poles, filled my water bottles, and hit the trail. My day's hike would be out from Rock Harbor, past Three-Mile Camp, and on to Daisy Farm. The total distance of this hike was a hair more than seven miles.

If you have hiked on Isle Royale you realize that hiking out to Daisy Farm after departing from the *Ranger III* is a fairly common route. Some people get off the boat after its 5:00 PM arrival at Rock Harbor and simply grab a campsite or shelter at Rock Harbor with an eye toward getting an early start the next day. Other folks hike out to Three-Mile Camp and settle in there for the first night. Many make a stab at going on to Daisy Farm as I planned to do. Some intrepid souls continue on along the Rock Harbor Trail to Moskey Basin four miles further down from Daisy Farm. Others go up the Mount Franklin Trail to the Greenstone Ridge, which acts as the spine of the main island. From that ridgeline those hikers can drop down to Lane Cove on the north shore of the park about seven miles from Rock Harbor. It is all in the eye of the beholder as each option is one that bears reason. I had done most of them and it really is a matter of personal preference. I had picked Daisy Farm and it was toward there that I walked.

My hike out to Daisy Farm was a very typical first trail day. Getting started on a backpacking trip involves breaking in your body, mind, spirit, and gear. Regardless of your training there is no substitute for hiking the actual ground with your gear in place. Try as you might, you simply cannot duplicate hiking a tough trail so you might as well prepare yourself for the need to work up to trail shape over a few days or so.

As has been my past experience, the thrill of being back in a beloved park gave me an immediate energy boost. For the first mile or so I felt charged by the exhilaration of being back to a place that I had been thinking about off and on all year. What a rush it was to be in a wilderness area once again!

After a while the reality of pack weight, changing terrain, temperatures much warmer than anticipated, and some lessened self-confidence began to tire me. The first three miles of the Rock Harbor Trail are easily underestimated. While there are no significant elevation changes there is an almost continuous washboard aspect to the stony landscape. The trail is also filled with rocks and exposed roots. If you plan on hiking this stretch of trail you will be blessed with some lovely shoreline views of Lake Superior and the outlying islands. You will also feel tired when you reach camp.

At Three-Mile I took a short five to ten minute break along the shore. I drank a half-liter of Gatorade and swatted some of the many mosquitoes that were out. The day was lovely but the park had obviously been going through a wet spell. Linked to a rise in temperature, the conditions were perfect for a large mosquito hatch. Nature looks for balance and these conditions called for a full-blown "baby boomer" generation of biting insects.

After taking a break I packed up and headed on toward Daisy Farm. To my left was Mott Island, home of the park's headquarters. This island is named after Charlie and Angelique Mott. Charlie Mott was an employee of a copper mining company that functioned on the island in the mid-19th century. Apparently Charlie and Angelique Mott were left to watch over the mining company's property one winter. Their supervisor swore that he would either return with adequate supplies for winter or arrange for their dispatch. As all too often happens in the working world, the Mott's boss was a selfish and addle pated person. No supplies were sent & the Motts were left to starve.

Apparently Charlie Mott began eyeing his wife in a way that struck Angelique as predatory. Before Mr. Mott could strike his spouse down and, quite probably, consume her, Charlie died of starvation and exposure. His wife was tempted to partake of her husband but chose instead to preserve his frozen body in a nearby shed. Mrs. Mott then made snares from her hair in which she managed to trap just enough snowshoe hares to survive until an early spring relief party arrived from the mainland. Hence, in honor of this couple's macabre experiences the park service named an island after them.

My hike in to Daisy Farm was relatively uneventful. I saw several loons & heard elements of their haunting calls. For me, there is no other sound, save the rarely heard howling of wolves, that captures the spirit of the Northwoods more fully than loon music. Aside from the aforementioned loons my only other wildlife observations on the trail were a few toads, one hare, and a group of raucous ravens that called and called across the bay.

Shortly before arriving in camp I saw the Rock Harbor Lighthouse and the small fishery buildings that are on the island that sits directly across the harbor from Daisy Farm. There were a few people in camp, which was not surprising, as Daisy Farm tends to be one of the busier campgrounds in the park. But, I had no trouble getting shelter number eleven where I gratefully settled in.

There are few feelings in life as sensually satisfying as dropping your backpack after a day's hike. Even if you have been careful & packed fairly light, backpacking over uneven ground will test you. Therefore, even though hiking with its sights & sounds is a great pastime, it usually is quite a relief to drop your pack and settle into camp.

The shelters at Isle Royale are a rather unique feature. Shelters are a cross between a screened-in porch and a mini-cabin. The shelters go on a first-come-first-served basis. However, in bad weather it is poor form to refuse to share a shelter with other hikers if they ask to. In all the days my hiking partners & I have been on Isle Royale we have had little difficulty securing a shelter in June at the campgrounds where they are available. We have also never had to share a shelter with strangers although we have offered to do so.

If you come to Isle Royale and stay in a shelter you have two major responsibilities. One is to sweep the shelter clean with the broom that each one is equipped with prior to your departure. The other responsibility is to keep your camp clean and tidy. Foxes, gray jays, red squirrels, ravens, and other critters patrol the camps looking for scraps & unguarded possessions. Feeding these animals is strictly forbidden by park regulations as it habituates patterns of behavior that endangers both the animals and the safety of other hikers. Likewise, unless you would like to see your camera, boot, water bottle, or other gear stolen away by animals, keep them secure.

After cooking some Mountain House spaghetti and a hot chocolate I set about doing a few camp chores. Water was filtered. Wet clothes were hung out. My sleeping bag and pad were laid out. My journaling ensued while the calls of seagulls competed with the playful sounds of children who were gathered down by the dock. I felt good about the day and looked forward to tomorrow's hike up and over the Greenstone Ridge, down past East Chickenbone Lake, and on to camp at McCargoe Cove on the north side of the island.

Hiking Tips:
#1: Prepare Yourself Physically & Mentally For Your Journey – Before heading out onto the trail you should dedicate time to working your fitness level up to a point where you can enjoy the experience of hiking. A

lack of training can lead to injury or disillusionment on the trail. Likewise, be realistic in terms of what you hope to accomplish on a trip. One's attitude to adversity can determine how a hike is perceived.

#2: Set & Honor your own Pace – No two people hike exactly the same trail. Your pace is your own and not to be judged by others. Factors such as weather, terrain, mood, and spirit will affect your pace. Be aware of how your body is performing and adjust to that reality. Hike the hike you need to and not what someone else expects. Be careful to avoid over or under ambitious trip goals.

#3: Watch Your Fluid Intake – If you are noticeably perspiring or feel fatigued, take periodic trail breaks and drink fluids. You do not want to dehydrate or suffer from heat exhaustion. On Isle Royale you have a ready water source available in the form of Lake Superior. But, on a hot day on one of the ridgelines, temperatures can be warmer by ten degrees or more than along the shore. On the ridges water can also be very scarce. Drink periodically throughout the day and filter up your bottles when opportunities present themselves.

#4: Listen More & Talk Less – While a big part of hiking can be comradeship, it can be profitable to talk less and more quietly than usual on the trail. By being quiet you can increase your chances of seeing wildlife. Use your time in camp or during trail breaks for big league conversations. On the trail try to attune yourself to nature's sights, sounds, tastes, and smells.

#5: Use Two Hiking Poles – Over the years as a hiker I have become firmly convinced that two hiking poles are far better than one. Using two poles eases pressure on your back, knees, and ankles. With a pair of trekking poles a hiker can be more stable on wet rocks, boggy terrain, or during stream crossings. On trail ascents and descents having two poles in hand can enhance stability. On flat ground a hiker can really dig in and motor with two poles serving the same purpose they do for a cross-country skier. It takes a bit of time to get used to coordinating two poles but the return on that investment of effort is great indeed!

#6: People Are Part of the Landscape Too – When hiking always be courteous to others. Keep your speaking tones down in camp. Do not let privy or shelter doors slam behind you. Greet other people and chat with them if there is a mutual inclination to do so. Yes, you probably went into a remote wilderness to get away from things, but so did most of the other folks you run into. Treat others with the same respect you accord to the wilderness locale you have chosen to visit and you will feel much better about your experience.

#7: Stay on Durable Surfaces – Either in camp or on the trail stay on designated & developed surfaces. The impact people can have on relatively delicate environments can be severe. Stay on the trail rather than widening it by avoiding minor mudholes or boggy areas. Camp only in designated sites unless you have a backcountry permit. Avoid crushing vegetation by camping in areas not set up for that purpose. Use the park in the way it was intended & help protect it for future visitors and current inhabitants.

Day 2 (Saturday—June 18): I got up early and had a couple granola bars & some dried fruit for breakfast. After packing up my gear and sweeping out the shelter I was ready to hit the trail at about 7:00 AM Eastern Time. The day was lovely and trails beckoned to me.

My goal for today was to cut up, along, and over the Greenstone Ridge and then descend to McCargoe Cove. The Greenstone is the longest of several ridgelines that help structure Isle Royale. Glaciers carved these ridges millenniums ago. This grinding action of ice on earth &

rock has resulted in some beautiful vistas and challenging climbs.

It was another sunny day with unusually high temperatures. The humidity was also up as evidenced by the heavy dew that coated the vegetation. The dew and the voluminous sweat that was pouring off my body quickly soaked me. It would be a day where I would need to closely monitor my fluid intake.

The first two miles leading up to the Greenstone went through several marshy areas. These bog lands featured long boardwalks that required some care to cross. An interesting beaver pond was passed but no moose were in sight. Once again the mosquitoes were fierce so I chose to don my head net. I was to use this useful mesh product off and on throughout the day.

When I reached the intersection with the Greenstone Ridge Trail I took a brief water break at a rocky overlook. In the distance I could see the Canadian shore. To my left Chickenbone Lake sat in a valley. As I sat there it really struck me what a powerful and beautiful sight I was seeing.

As I drank some Gatorade I heard an odd noise in the distance. At first I thought it was a morning whistle from some distant factory in Thunder Bay over on the Canadian shore. Then, in a few seconds, I realized that what I was listening to was wolf howls from a valley down toward the north shore of the island and McCargoe Cove. I froze and listened as the wolves howled and barked. Each set of howls was started by a simple bark. The wolves then moved on to the classic & drawn out chorus that we associate with these wild creatures. Standing on the rocky bluff, listening to the wild calls of the wolves, I felt in awe.

As I stood on the Greenstone, early in the morning while the wolves howled in the distance, I fully understood why I keep coming back to this place. The trails a hiker uses on Isle Royale are also used by the wolf packs that live there. To hear some of the island's wolves is a rare privilege & one I have treasured each time good fortune has smiled on me and allowed me to hear them.

Moving on from that magic moment I headed along the Greenstone for about four miles. The terrain was up and down with few long-range views. Most of this stretch of the ridge was a walk in the woods with occasional glimpses of Lake Superior in the distance.

As I followed the Greenstone I looked up at one point and saw a multi-colored fox in the path ahead of me. The fox was startled by me but did not flee. Instead it sat down and stared at me. I spoke to the fox in quiet tones and it cocked its head much as our family dogs do back home when they try to understand human speech. The fox and I were separated by about twenty feet as we studied one another. The brownish yellow irises of the fox's eyes almost glistened as it tried to figure me out.

After a bit of communing with the trail fox I moved on. The morning was becoming steadily warmer and I had to stop to wring out my headbands several times. I also found myself drinking more fluids than I usually do on a trip to the park. As the day wore on I struggled to maintain my hydration. I was struck by how unseasonably warm and humid it was this early in the Isle Royale hiking season.

At East Chickenbone Camp I headed down the descending spur trail that leads to McCargoe Cove. This two-mile stretch is usually wet and buggy and this year was no exception. Plant growth was pronounced and made it difficult to negotiate some of the many boardwalks. Sections of the planking were completely hidden by ferns and other plants. This circumstance called for greater caution and attention to the trail.

As I tried to maneuver along one particularly muddy patch I lost my balance and ended up falling into the muck. When I got up I felt foolishly dirty, but also unhurt. If you go into the woods with any regularity to hike you will occasionally fall. The key is to be careful and bounce back.

Not too far down the spur trail heading toward McCargoe I saw a pileated woodpecker fly right past me. These crow-sized birds were the original models for the animated "Woody the Woodpecker" who behaved so badly in both comic books and on television. Seeing one in the wild is a rare treat and one to be valued. The pileated woodpecker's striking red, black, and white coloration and their loud "Kuk, kuk, kuk…" call makes them a memorable inhabitant of the Northwoods.

As I neared McCargoe Cove I had to admit that I felt fatigued. I was drenched with sweat and it was dripping off of my face. As I entered the camp area I saw four people sitting near the fire ring. We exchanged helloes and one of the women asked me if my drenched clothes were the result of water or perspiration. I responded by saying, "A little of both." I then excused myself in order to grab a shelter and drop my pack.

Once again, the sensation of pronounced relief that comes from taking off your pack after the day's hike can only be understood by those people who have felt it. I stripped off my soiled clothes and changed into my dry camp wear. I laid out my gear and took a rest. After a while I cooked a dehydrated meal of chicken and rice along with a double hot chocolate. Lying out soaked gear to dry in the sun followed lunch. I then attended to filtering water, washing muck off my tired body, and soaking my unblistered feet in the cove.

As always, there were a number of fellow campers at McCargoe Cove. This site sits at the end of a long finger-like cove that points in from the island's rugged north shore. McCargoe is a beautiful spot where wildlife abounds. In the past I have seen a number of moose, loons, Merganser ducks, nesting turtles, eagles, and otters here. Numerous birds and butterflies often flit around the camp area. I have also heard wolves howling here, as it is part of the territory of the Chippewa Harbor pack. However, McCargoe Cove is also an intersection for canoeists, hikers, boaters, park service boats, and the *Voyageur II.* So, if you plan on staying at McCargoe Cove after early June and before September, you will have company.

While I was lying in the cool shelter I noticed a bird nest up in the rafters of the overhang that shaded the front part of the structure. A pair of white-throated song sparrows was flying back and forth, feeding their chicks. Every time one of the hard working parents returned with an insect or other food, tiny heads emerged from the nest and loudly pleaded. Birds are generally dedicated parents. Watching the song sparrows reminded me of my own responsibilities as the father of three children.

People can sometimes learn great lessons through observing animal behavior. In nature, the care of the young is the paramount responsibility of most species. The song sparrows that tirelessly fed their chicks or a moose mother who stands her ground to defend her calf from the wolves are but two examples of how many animal parents risk everything for their young. Thinking of those behaviors I felt both kinship and appreciation for the selfless song sparrow parents who worked and worked to raise their family.

As the day drew to a close I spent time down by the fire ring talking to people. A family from Naperville, Illinois, which is fairly close to my hometown of DeKalb, was there. The husband was an airline pilot and his ambitious middle school aged daughter was planning out the next day's hike. The wife was a very well read & thoughtful conversationalist. It is generally amazing how many fundamentally good people you can meet in a place like Isle Royale. But is this reality really so surprising? Would you not expect to run into folks who are less materialistic, more environmentally minded, and interested in nature's bounty in a remote wilderness park? Part of my solo journey was the pursuit and study of solitude. But, humans are social beings and today's conversations were much appreciated.

Hiking Tips:

#8: Learn How to Fall – An occasional fall is part and parcel of backpacking. A key is to take falls as seldom as possible and in as controlled a manner as you can. If you slip and fall on the trail try to turn into the direction of your fall so that your pack can absorb as much of the impact as possible. On ascents lean into the climb and be prepared to brace yourself with your hiking poles and arms rather than landing face first. On descents take your time and position your weight & feet so that you can turn a fall into a "sit down" rather than a headfirst cascade down a rocky slope.

#9: When Crossing Boardwalks Pay Strict Attention – Boardwalks are a gift made possible by the diligence and effort of NPS workers. These park employees bridge marshes, bogs, and wet areas that otherwise would be either impossible or miserable to cross. Boardwalks can be slippery and partially concealed by plants. When crossing any of the park's many boardwalks pay attention to every step. Make it a cardinal rule to walk and not gawk when traversing boardwalks. If you want to check out a nearby beaver pond or marsh area for wildlife, stop, stand still, and look without taking a risk. I have seen several people fall off boardwalks because they were trying to do too many things at once. Do not follow this example and stay dry.

#10: Do Not Underestimate the Trail – Isle Royale does not feature towering mountains like the Smokies or Rockies. What the park does feature is a roller coaster landscape, many wet areas, lots of rocks and roots, and trail sections that are only obscure paths across basalt. Do not make the mistake of underestimating these trails. Sections of the ridge trails can be very tough going. Be prepared for slick rocks, ascents that will test your endurance, grinding descents, and wet boots.

#11: Do Not Rush Through the End of the Day's Hike – There is a natural tendency to surge ahead when you get near camp at the end of the day. Try to suppress this urge. Vince Lombardi, the late great coach of the Green Bay Packers football team, once said, "Fatigue makes fools of us all." A tired mind and body are more prone to mistakes than a fresh one. At the end of a day's hike you probably are dealing with some level of fatigue. To rush down the trail in that circumstance is to invite error. Many of my worst falls have come near the end of a hiking day. Hold back a bit and try to concentrate even harder as you near camp. In this way you increase the likelihood of reaching camp without mishap or injury.

#12: Wear Quick Drying Clothing – On the trail the clothes you wear will get saturated with moisture from many sources. You will sweat and drench your clothing. Rain will fall from the heavens and soak you. Dew covered plants will dampen you. If you wear wicking socks, shirts, pants, and shorts you stand a decent chance of drying out your stuff in a reasonable time period. If, on the other hand, you choose to wear jeans, cotton socks, traditional tee shirts, sweatshirts, or other non-wicking fabrics, you will have a lump of heavy, wet clothing that will remained soaked all trip. Use modern, quick drying clothing and you will enjoy your hiking experience far more.

#13: Repackage Your Foodstuffs in Zip-lock Baggies – There is no reasonable need to bring 95% or more of the packaging your food comes in with you when you backpack. Recycle the plastic and cardboard packaging that your raisins, dried fruit, granola bars, Gatorade, crackers, bagels, or other pre-packaged foods come in. Transfer them into baggies & reduce both garbage in your pack and the space needed for your food bag.

#14: Bring Toilette Paper – While privies are available at each park campground, and they generally have toilette paper, you cannot always count on that fact of life. Also, bodies are unpredictable and the calls of nature can come at the most inconvenient times. Pack a compressed half-roll of toilette paper in a baggie with you. It weighs virtually nothing and will be valued if and when it is needed.

#15: Do Not Miss the Trail Experience because You are Looking for One Thing – Many people come to Isle Royale with one goal—to see moose. They tramp along solely looking for moose only to miss many other wonders. As you walk note the toads, slugs, and snails below. Listen for the subtle yet lovely calls of the song sparrows. Watch for red squirrels, foxes, and woodpeckers. Moose will be seen if they are meant to be seen. You can maximize your chances of seeing moose by realizing that they feel uncomfortable when the temperature rises above forty-five degrees. In warmer weather they seek out water or ruminate in shady areas. Hit the trail early, quietly observe beaver ponds & lakes, watch for moose in the evening, and try to hike quietly. However, be aware of all the other types of life that surround you as well.

Day 3 (Sunday—June 19): Today is both a clear and beautiful day as well as Father's Day. I awoke very early at about 5:30 AM Eastern Time. Lying in my sleeping bag I felt somewhat fatigued from the first two days on the island's trails. I was also a little apprehensive concerning my sleeping arrangements over the next two days.

As a solo hiker in order to keep my pack weight as low as possible I had left my tent back home. Instead, I substituted a lightweight tarp as a means of meeting my shelter needs. This substitution resulted in my saving a few pounds of pack weight. Back in Illinois this arrangement made perfect sense. Now, out on the island in a year when the mosquito hatch was ample, I was concerned about being sucked into anemia.

In planning this trip I had counted on getting a shelter at six of the eight camps I would visit. In June most of the campgrounds, and in particular those located on the western half of the park, are generally sparsely populated with hikers. This year I had already noticed a larger than usual number of backpackers and boaters. Perhaps the warm weather had inspired some of the boaters or impulse hikers to come out? Whatever the reason I could not count on getting shelters as easily as in past years.

With that thought in mind I decided that the key would be getting as early a start as possible every day in order to make camp in the morning rather than later in the day. In this way I might stand a better chance of getting a shelter while also having more opportunity to read, write, explore, and have some down time.

Today's hiking plan was to head down the first section of the Minong Trail from McCargoe Cove to Todd Harbor. There was only one shelter at Todd Harbor and, from listening to people in camp at McCargoe Cove, I knew there were several hikers headed there today. Todd Harbor is a jewel of a place. The harbor opens up to a view of the Canadian islands and shore. On clear days Todd Harbor features stunning and colorful sunsets.

Moose often come through camp. Loons populate the harbor and frequently call out. This was a place I really wanted to get to early enough to both appreciate it and bed down in the comfort of its solo shelter.

I broke camp at McCargoe Cove at about 6:00 AM and hit the trail. I had hiked the full length of the Minong a number of times and in both an easterly and westerly direction. The Minong Trail stretches from McCargoe Cove to Windigo at the western end of the park. For about thirty-five miles hikers are treated to what many people consider one of the premier hikes available not only in the park but also throughout the Midwest.

Originally set up as a firefighter's trail, the Minong is much more challenging than the entire park's other trails. Progressively, across its four sections, the Minong can wear down an unprepared hiker. The trail features numerous ascents and descents that will test endurance and jar bones. Streams must be crossed and some of them can be tricky. Some sections of the trail, and in particular the portion leading up to North Desor Camp, are ill defined. These vague parts of the trail lead the hiker out onto unforgiving sections of basaltic stone that can be both unclear to follow and hard on feet. In the final thirteen-mile segment from North Desor to Windigo hikers climb about a dozen hills of more than one hundred feet. In that part of the Minong backpackers also cross three beaver dams, several wet areas, and a floating log section that, in wet years, can be a pathway to a boot soaking. If you choose to hike the Minong be prepared for a walking experience that is a cut above the difficulty of other portions of the park.

Conversely, although the Minong Trail is tough it holds great rewards within itself as well. Those intrepid souls who hike out on the Minong will be afforded some beautiful memories. The ridgeline views of Lake Superior and Canada beyond are lovely. Fewer hikers take the

Minong so there is far more privacy than in some other parts of the park. Wildlife viewing can be quite good and there are a fair number of moose in this territory. Wolves traverse this part of the park with some regularity. So, a careful observer can often find their scat, tracks, or pieces of fur. The higher difficulty of parts of the Minong is a reward in itself. If you hike the Minong well, you will remember it and learn from that experience.

Heading out on the first seven-mile section of the Minong I looked forward to revisiting a trail that had given me so much in the past. This initial section of the Minong was my least favorite of the four. The ground had some beautiful spots but there tended to be some "sameness" to much of the trail. Yet, there were also some nice stretches of birch woods and rocky bluffs to climb. With those thoughts in mind I still considered this hike a fine one.

The first mile or so out of McCargoe takes a hiker through a fairly open forest. A few wet spots in the trail called for judgment and patience but in general the trail was fairly level with many opportunities to look out into the surrounding woods. Slightly less than a mile into the walk a spur trail heads down into a valley where the remains of the old Minong Mine can be observed. I took the spur and went down to take a look at some of the water-filled mining pits and piles of rock tailings. Using hand tools, picks, shovels, and black powder, these mid-19th century miners exerted Herculean effort to try to make a go of their mining operations. Amid changeable weather, biting insects, rugged terrain, and isolation these hearty miners ultimately failed. Isle Royale was simply too remote to make its mineral bounty profitable enough to warrant the effort needed to extract and market it. The mines winked out and all that now remains of all that backbreaking work are the pits and mine leavings.

After looking around for a bit I headed back up the spur trail to the main intersection. A note of caution, if you do not want to look at the mine and find yourself heading sharply down off the ridge at the one mile point—stop and retrace your steps. There is no trail marker indicating where the mine spur begins. Also, the point where the spur heads downhill is a rather obscure point. The trail is narrow and somewhat hidden by grasses. So, keep your eyes open or backtrack. Otherwise you will find yourself dead-ending at the mine site only to have to grunt your way back up the ridge.

From the mine spur on for about two miles the trail periodically headed up along the rocky eminence of the ridge. Some of the climbs up to the ridgeline were moderate while others were fairly steep. If you find yourself hiking this part of the Minong in the rain or on a damp day take care on the rocky portions of the trail, as they can be extremely slippery. This slippage factor is particularly true during ascents and descents where particular attention should be paid to footing.

This portion of the trail allowed for some fine views of the big lake and was lovely. Coming out onto the open patches where vistas of Lake Superior were available was wonderful. A cooling north wind helped a great deal. Nevertheless I found myself watching sweat dripping off my nose and chin onto the rocks below my trudging feet.

As I hiked this stretch I could feel the weight of some of life's pressures and depression slipping away. Every year that I come up to Isle Royale I feel as if this wilderness setting offers me a spiritual bath. The beauty and effort that are part of an Isle Royale experience scrubs away the residue, grime, & sadness that can accumulate over the year at work. In a way, my journey north is an annual pilgrimage that features a rebirth of hope.

About three miles into the hike the trail downshifts and becomes a rolling walk in the woods. When the path breaks back onto the ridge, diminutive Otter Lake can be seen down in a valley to the north. This woodland lake is one of the few landmarks hikers can use to gauge their daily progress. Once you pass Otter Lake you are about 40% of the way to Todd Harbor.

After Otter Lake I encountered essentially a hilly & pleasant woods walk. Portions of the trail went through tall birch woods. The white and silvery bark of these trees stood out while their green leaves danced in the breezes above my head. The birch woods parts of the Minong are both lovely and ethereal.

As I approached the final third of the trail I finally broke down and donned my mosquito mesh. Too many little dive-bombers were going for my ears, eyes, and face. I appreciate netting for its protective properties but it does complicate some aspects of trail life. The mesh mars your view of the woods and, under certain lighting conditions, can screen your vision. Mosquito mesh makes your body's ability to exchange heat slightly less effective, as it is somewhat smothering. Hence, when you wear a head net you may well experience more profuse facial sweating. Mosquito netting can also cause some inconvenience in terms of mopping your brow or blowing your nose. However, it is an inexperienced or foolish hiker who visits Isle Royale without mesh. Further, I cannot remember any trip to the park where my trail partner or I did not use mesh at some point. Perhaps fall hiking would be an exception to this truism but the miniscule weight of a head net is certainly something a wise hiker will be able to manage under any circumstances.

The next landmark to look for on this part of the Minong is Lake Harvey. Although hikers do not get a clear look at the lake they will see beaver ponds and the forest depression where the lake sits. You can bushwhack over for a look at the lake but it is not recommended due to the marshy areas that surround much of its shore. Once you notice Lake Harvey you are within range of Todd Harbor. At the lake's end you will cross a stream on some rocks and head into the final three-quarters of a mile or so of your hike. On this day I felt particularly strong at this point and surged up the trail. A few minor hills ensued but I felt determined to get to camp and, hopefully, snag the shelter.

In the final stretch I encountered the only hikers I met that day on the trail. First a father and his young son passed me heading toward McCargoe. Then, perhaps a half-mile later, a mother with two other youngsters came along. This family group looked well outfitted and seemed to be veterans of the trail. It was refreshing to see a family out tramping in the woods. Perhaps these parents, like my own years ago, can pass those interests and values on to their children? Based on today's observation they seemed to be heading in the right direction.

As I neared camp I could see snippets of Lake Superior through the trees. A refreshing breeze off the lake was quite bracing. The trail began to be littered with rocks that I recalled was evidence of the age old shifting of the Lake Superior shoreline. Those rocks were also a sure sign that I was near Todd Harbor. Just before reaching camp I came to a narrow stream. After hopping over that rivulet I came around a corner and entered camp. Much to my enjoyment I found the single shelter empty and available.

Quickly, I changed out of my soaked trail clothing and into camp garb. As at McCargoe Cove I used the camp picnic table as a drying wrack. In short order my home away from home was established and set up. Sitting on my sleeping bag, in dry clothes with a warm cup of soup in my hand, I felt like a king.

Once I was in camp it was time for a rest. Today's pacing was good and I felt stronger on the trail than either of the two previous days. I made the seven miles from McCargoe in about two hours and fifteen minutes. In camp I felt less drained than yesterday. Over a period of days my trail conditioning should steadily improve and help me finish up in good order.

An hour or so after my arrival other hikers began to come into camp. First came Don from Milwaukee, an avid backpacker who had previously through-hiked the Appalachian Trail in 1996. Next came a husband and wife team from a small town near Grand Rapids, Michigan. Both of these cheerful folks were schoolteachers out enjoying the start of their summer vacation. Later, a large group of boys trudged through and on to the group campsites across the harbor. Another couple and a family of three also pulled in. The number of people who I saw out on the island in June amazed me.

In terms of wildlife it was a somewhat limited day. There were still no moose in sight but that was not entirely surprising. Moose numbers were down to about 580. To put this number in perspective, there were about 1500 moose on the island five years ago. A combination of weather, tick infestations, and increasing wolf numbers has taken a toll on the moose. Therefore, fewer moose mean less likelihood of seeing them.

I did see quite a number of wolf prints along the first three to four miles of the Minong. Some of the prints were very distinct and looked almost like artistic plaster casts. Later, in camp, I heard and saw loons. A mated pair of Merganser ducks patrolled the harbor while raucous seagulls called. A bald eagle flew overhead and triggered both a loon alarm call and threat displays by the Mergansers.

Today being Father's Day, made me think about my late father & my role as a parent. In the middle of Isle

Royale it may have seemed strange to reflect on such a broad subject but part of heading off on an excursion like this one is to learn about your self. Thus, in honor of my father who was a staunch environmentalist, and my own three children each of whom is a decent and precious person, I sat down and wrote out the following lessons drawn from wild places such as Isle Royale:

1. All life is important and worthy of respect.
2. It is far easier to destroy than to build.
3. Courage has little to do with power and much to do with character.
4. Through perseverance in the face of adversity victories can be won even after defeats.
5. Preparation is more of a factor in success than either luck or natural talent.
6. Wilderness is both a physical place & a spiritual mindset.
7. The test of hard trails, wet days, & taxing climbs build both physical and moral strength.
8. Memories drawn from nature can replenish you when life droops.
9. Personal growth achieved via wilderness outings must translate to improvement in relationships & behavior, or it is hollow.
10. No one unfamiliar with the places you visit will fully understand the experiences you have had—so do not be disappointed & share what you can.

As Father's Day, as well as another day on the island, came to a close, I felt comfortable. It is a good day when you can hike in the woods, set up a cozy camp, converse with thoughtful people, spend time reading, and look out on a beautiful setting. It is times like this that can sustain a person in the periods of trial that occur in virtually everyone's life. There is regeneration in life and wilderness can be a part of that rebuilding process.

Hiking Tips:

#16: Avoid Cross Over Steps – Sometimes, on the trail, and in particular on ascents & descents, there is a temptation to cross one foot in front of the other in order to avoid an obstacle. Try to avoid this temptation, as cross over strides can be the source of bad falls. As you cross one foot in front of the other all you need do is stub your toe on a rock, slip a bit, or lose your balance, and you will trip yourself. Nature offers enough hazards on the trail without creating more of our own. Try to keep knees and ankles in line and you will have a much more stable center of gravity.

#17: Never Rush Stream Crossing – If you hike any distance on Isle Royale, or elsewhere, you will cross streams. If the crossing point features rocks and downed logs be careful to check each step for stability before committing to it. Make use of your two hiking sticks to balance & support your body. Take your time & concentrate as you cross. If you have to wade be careful of slippery rocks or deeper holes in the streambed. Again, use your poles to stabilize yourself and check for holes. Never underestimate a stream crossing. Take your time— it is not a race to be won. A mistake on a stream crossing can result in bad results ranging from a dousing to even death.

#18: Do Not Collect Souvenirs – At Isle Royale you will encounter the temptation to take home a keepsake of your trip. Bits of rock, moose bones, and other wood & shoreline elements may seem tempting as potential shelf decorations. Never follow through on these desires. The park exists as a valued ecosystem. It has been set aside as a refuge for both its inhabitants and visitors. Honor this place, and other parks, by taking only memories away with you. It is possible to love a place to death. Show respect for the park and leave it as it is.

#19: Follow Your Daily Rhythm – A solid back-packing experience calls for planning and preparation. You really cannot "throw together" a trip to this place and do it justice. You also should have some sort of planned itinerary in mind inclusive of goals and mileage targets. However, how fast you walk, what you do in camp, whether you choose to explore or rest, and how much you wish to interact with others is your choice. Remember that you are on a vacation. So long as you are considerate of others and the land, you should follow your own daily rhythms.

#20: Bring Reading Materials – Time in camp can be an opportunity to catch up with a favorite novel or other genre of book. Carefully select your reading material so that the wilderness setting you are visiting can be complemented by it. Also beware of the temptation to bring too many books with you in your pack. Every ounce you carry will impact upon your body with each step you take. Be judicious in your book selection & reflect upon the appropriate content to supplement your trip. But bring reading materials and enjoy the chance to reflect on them in the wild.

Day 4 (Monday—June 20): Today I awoke to an overcast and grim looking sky. While overcast can be a distinct advantage when hiking on Isle Royale's ridges, I was concerned about the timing of potential rain. My day's destination was South Desor where I would be sleeping under my tarp. Rain on my first tarp day was unwelcome to say the least. But, one thing that is certainly true is that life is what it is. Only people intent upon creating their own unhappiness will look at life's realities and pine for their own unattainable wishes. You have to play the cards dealt to you to have any chance of enjoying the game.

As I began to change into my grubby hiking clothes and pack up for the day, Ben & Rose, the two teachers from Grand Haven stopped by the shelter to bid me farewell. Both of these folks were very kind and personable. We wished each other good luck on our respective journeys. Ben and Rose were headed up the Minong while I was skirting Hatchet Lake and then heading down the Greenstone Ridge to South Lake Desor.

I broke camp around 7:00 and started up the Minong to the trail intersection with the path leading on to Hatchet Lake. I had previously hiked this way so I had a fair knowledge of the terrain. The short stretch of the Minong that I took that day was very level and generally featured open forest. The gray morning seemed to weigh heavily on my mind but I tried to focus on the hike and not what the weather might do. A key to successful hiking, or many aspects of life in general, is to be able to focus on the present moment & enjoy it to the greatest extent possible. Thinking about rain, tarps, bugs, and doubts was taking me out of a positive mindset. To combat this I consciously slowed my pace a bit, watched my foot placements with greater focus, and tried to observe what I could of the land I was traveling through.

In a relatively short period of time I came to the Hatchet Lake spur trail. As I turned on to it a drizzle began to fall. Although the rain was not heavy it continued as a steady factor as it fell on me for me next hour. In that time the rain also managed to soak the ferns, thimbleberries, and other undergrowth that closely hugged the narrow trail. As a result my clothing, boots, and socks were quickly drenched. I was to remain wet for the rest of this hiking day.

The Hatchet Lake Trail runs on for about 2.3 miles. It features a few climbs and some pleasing forest scenery. This is a densely forested path that heads up to the lake and then generally hugs its shore before finally ending at the campground. Hatchet Lake is a moderately sized backwoods lake. The camp is pleasant but can be rather buggy. As I was not planning on staying at Hatchet I dropped my pack for only a break. The day was very humid so I drank a liter of water and refilled my bottle from the lake. As I filtered literally hundreds of mosquitoes flew around me. Needless to say, I did not stay in that spot too long.

Heading out of Hatchet Lake up to the Greenstone Ridge affords a hiker an opportunity to make one of the steeper climbs in the entire park. The four tenths of a mile that it takes to reach the ridgeline is essentially a head-on climb of hundreds of feet in elevation gain. There are several switchbacks but this climb will get even the fittest hiker's heart and lungs working.

At the top of the hill I felt very strong. As I headed west toward Lake Desor I began to think about walking all the way to Windigo. The thought of a shelter on Washington Creek where moose are often sighted got my mind thinking about a cumulative twenty-three mile day. With gray skies overhead I started along the Greenstone with no definite destination but several possibilities in mind.

The Greenstone Ridge from Hatchet Lake to Desor encompasses generally level to rolling terrain. There are some hills that increase respiration but much of the trail is flat or moderate in nature. The hiker goes through woody sections with undergrowth crowding the trail. Indeed, while there are some open spots where long-range views are available, these are few and far between.

As I hiked through the dense ferns I felt very solid in terms of my trail conditioning. My feet were fine and my pack was much lighter than at the start of the trip. The idea of hiking on to Windigo became increasingly cemented in my mind as a reasonable option.

About halfway to Desor I came to the Ishpeming Tower. This relatively low structure is used for meteorological studies conducted by park staff. It also served as a good place for me to take my trail break.

After dropping my pack I was promptly attacked by numerous mosquitoes. Despite these creatures best efforts my handy bug spray kept them off and allowed me to have a reasonably relaxing break. I took off my boots, wrung out my socks, and pulled out a granola bar and some pecans for a snack. Just as I started to eat some hikers arrived from the opposite direction.

The group was part of a Boy Scout outing from Cary, Illinois. The group leader, Gary, was in charge of his son and two other youngsters. These folks were in their fourth day of a long hike that included the Feldtmann Ridge Trail and parts of the Greenstone, Minong, and Rock Harbor Trails. We chatted for about fifteen minutes or so and then I departed. Once again, the community of the trail was both appreciated and good-natured. It is well worth the effort to talk to folks if they appear to welcome conversation.

From the Ishpeming Tower I headed on toward Lake Desor. By now the skies had cleared and the temperature was steadily rising. Up on the ridge I could feel warmth radiating up at me from both the ground and the sun above. The undergrowth was drying but I was still soaked, albeit now from perspiration.

As I neared the spur trail to Desor I had already decided to head on into camp to at least cook lunch, drink water, and replenish my liquids. When I finally reached Desor trail I felt somewhat bushed. I had already covered twelve miles and the day was cooking up. Desor is a lovely spot and I had always enjoyed staying there. My feet were also mildly complaining to me about rocks and other hard features of the trail. Putting all of these factors together I decided to call it a day. I felt I could have pushed on to Windigo but to what end and at what cost?

With no one else in camp I chose the furthest west site. I quickly rigged out my tarp in a way that reminded me of a Civil War soldier's primitive "shebang." Basically, I used a downed birch tree that was caught by other trees and leaning at a forty-five degree angle as a ridgepole. I draped my tarp over the downed birch and secured its ends with rocks from camp. I then slipped my sleeping bag into a waterproof cover and laid it out on my pad under the tarp. Other belongings as well as my pack were secured under the protective tarp as well. I planned on using my coat to help cover my face and ward off insects.

Once camp was set I cooked my last dehydrated meal and enjoyed the stew. Water was then filtered and I spent some time looking at the lake. Lake Desor is one of the larger bodies of water on Isle Royale. It is essentially kidney-shaped and has several wooded islands within it. There are camps on both sides of the lake that afford hikers traveling on either the Greenstone or Minong Ridge Trails a pleasant place to stay. Desor is sharply blue on a clear day and stands out as one of the lovelier lakes in the park. Its water is cool and refreshing while also serving as a good place to soak tired feet.

Desor also is a place where campers are treated to living in a birch forest. All through the camps tall white and silver birch trees stretch up into the sky. The whitish bark and trembling leaves are inspiring. Camping by Desor on a good day is a treat and almost spiritual in nature. Visitors can be treated to large animals like moose coming through camp as well as smaller, yet still fascinating, creatures that live in and around the campsites. I spent several hours just looking out at the lake and watching the butterflies and other insects that populated my home away from home.

As my fourth day on the island came to a close I spent a very quiet evening alone. There were no other visible campers at Desor. I was glad to have camped there as the day became very hot. I had no way to gauge the temperature but, as I was sweating in camp even when I just lay down, I had to estimate it to have been at least ninety degrees. At that temperature four additional hours on the Greenstone would have been unnecessarily tough. I planned to cover them next morning when the air would be much cooler.

My afternoon and early evening at Desor were spent reading and doing camp chores. I always enjoy the books I bring on a hiking trip. Today I finished *To Kill A Mockingbird* by Harper Lee. What a wonderful story and so well told! It always amazes me that *To Kill A Mockingbird* was Lee's sole novel. The story of Atticus Finch, the crusading southern lawyer, and his two children—Jem & Scout—is universally valuable. In a place of peace and natural order it was refreshing to read a classic story wherein people search for decency in the human world.

I have also started and almost finished the Taoist classic the *Tao Te Ching* by Lao Tzu. This poetic and brief book offers insights into how to lead a balanced life. Perhaps by re-reading these words on this trip I could find new gems of knowledge from this keynote work?

As I sat with my journal in hand I decided to close out my day's entry with some pluses and minuses to solo hiking Isle Royale. After four days I had come to some first impressions of solo hiking in the park and some points of comparison may be valuable:

Pluses
1. Solo hikers set their own pace and can deviate from their itineraries with ease.
2. Hiking alone offers time for solitude and reflection.
3. A solo hiker disturbs the woods less and theoretically should have enhanced opportunities for wildlife observation.
4. Hiking alone leaves you responsible only for yourself and your own well-being.
5. Solo hiking builds up your independence and self-confidence.
6. Daily routines such as mealtimes, breaks, and chores can be scheduled and carried out as you wish.

Minuses
1. The solo hiker must carry everything he or she needs—there is no sharing of the load.
2. You are responsible for all camp chores.
3. You must be doubly careful, as you have no partners to help you in case of a mishap.
4. There is no trusted friend or comrade to share the day's events with.
5. You can get lonely.
6. There is no one else to help problem solve when the unexpected occurs.

Hiking Tips:
#21: Pack as Light as is Practicable – Every ounce that you carry exerts an effect upon your body for every moment that you bear its weight. When backpacking, you must have the essentials that you require for a safe and enjoyable experience. Each luxury item or non-essential object you take will impact upon your knees, ankles, back, and spirit with every step you take. Be reasonable

but also realistic when setting up your pack. There is no easier way to ruin a backpacking trip than to carry too much weight.

#22: Maintain a Journal – Many hikers keep a written journal of their trips. Writing on the trail can be a way to capture ideas, thoughts, inspirations, or questions that come to you on the trail or in camp. Journals can also be revisited at a later date in an effort to recall what you felt or did at a given time in life. Additionally journals can be good source books if you are planning on revisiting this, or other, parks. By looking back at a prior trip you may be better able to prepare for a future one. Finally, journals can be either kept as a private diary or shared with loved ones who did not accompany you on the trip.

#23: Pack Out What You Pack In – It can be demoralizing to hike long, hard miles to get to a remote place only to find trash strewn about. Show respect for the land & other visitors by packing out the trash you bring into the park with you. In addition, if you come upon other people's discarded litter, pack it out too. Leave Isle Royale, and other parks you travel to, better because of your presence rather than diminished.

#24: Bring Camp Shoes – At day's end your hiking boots may be soaked, mud-caked, or simply stifling. Once you are in camp it is strongly recommended that you have some sort of lightweight camp shoe to wear. Pool shoes, lightweight sandals, or ultra-light walking shoes are but a few examples of such camp footwear. In camp you will want relief from your boots. Be sure to bring a lightweight option to change into so your boots can dry & your feet can decompress.

#25: Try to Observe the Minute Life Around You – Every interesting wildlife observation need not involve a 1500-pound bull moose. On the trail, or in camp, you can see amazing things simply by looking around. Look down and watch ants carrying objects that dwarf them. Watching dragonflies hunting mosquitoes can be both fascinating and cathartic. Finding orchids, wild roses, or other wildflowers can be breathtaking. Having butterflies land on you and syringe off sweat from your arm is a gift. Try to notice and appreciate these subtle yet memorable happenings. Such careful observation can make your woodland journey a much more all-encompassing experience.

#26: Pack Layers of Clothing – Weather on Isle Royale can be justly compared to a mentally ill person suffering from multiple personalities. Sharp changes in temperature and sudden onsets of precipitation are the norm. Also, temperatures along the Lake Superior shore are far different than those achieved inland and along the high ridges. Bring layers of clothing that offer you the capability of dealing with the climate inconsistencies of Isle Royale's conditions.

#27: Think of Your Trip as a Journey & Not a Race - Sometimes there is a tendency among hikers to measure the value of a trip by how many miles were covered and not what was seen along the way. Everyone hikes their own hike and sets their own standards. But, is the goal of a trip to plow through as many miles as is humanly possibly, as quickly as possible, or is it to "see" the park? Think about that question and try to allow yourself a hiking itinerary that gives you permission to dawdle, explore, and pause in wonderment if you wish to.

Day 5 (Tuesday—June 21): You can learn from everything. Last night I learned that coming to Isle Royale in June with a tarp rather than a tent was a poor choice indeed! In past years when I visited the island June was generally a cool month with minimal bug problems. This year, the onset of summer-like weather, linked to some very wet spring weeks, led to the worst mosquito hatches

I had ever seen in the park. Hence, sleeping under a tarp was a miserable experience.

The previous evening had started out all right. Some clouds blew in but the sky was not threatening. However, once I had settled into my sleeping bag the mosquitoes began to swarm. I had planned to sleep under my mesh and burrow into my mummy bag but Mother Nature had other ideas. The evening was oppressively warm and humid, making my strategy a faulty one.

Every time I tried to pull into my sleeping bag, much like a turtle retreating into its shell, I quickly found myself stifling due to the unseasonable heat. In fact, it was so hot in my bag that, under normal circumstances, I would have slept on top of rather than in it. But, these were far from normal circumstances.

Hundreds of mosquitoes hovered and buzzed around my head. I tried a variety of strategies to cover up including using my raincoat to drape over my head, pulling my pack cover over me like a tarp, switching into my woolen sleeping cap with my mesh over the top, but nothing worked. Either I began to melt or the merciless creatures found a way to break through my defenses and bite me.

For hours I waged war with these infernal mosquitoes. No defense I created fully worked. Each time I popped out of my shell so to speak, I was overwhelmed by the clouds of biting pests that surrounded me. When I was undercover inevitably some of the biters would start chewing on my neck, back, or hands. When I covered up I could hear the beasts pecking away & buzzing. All in all this ranks as the worst night I have ever spent on the trail. Eventually, I took two liquid Nyquil capsules and drifted off for a couple hours of meager sleep. That night, while the mosquitoes buzzed and bit, I dreamed of a deer driven mad by biting insects.

I awoke at about 4:30 and immediately set about breaking camp. The mosquitoes were still around by the hundreds and attacked me as I changed into my grungy hiking clothes. I stuffed my pack in record time and hurriedly left Desor without breakfast or any backward looks. It felt great to leave that place after a night of misery.

My destination for the day was Windigo, about eleven and a half miles to the west. With little sleep, no breakfast, and some blood loss in the night I started out the day in slow motion. My body felt a bit leaden but I was still very happy to be out of the clutches of Lake Desor's mosquitoes.

Immediately after leaving the spur trail I was confronted by the first of several climbs that were prominent in the stretch of trail going from Desor to Island Mine. The rocky ridges were covered with wildflowers many of which would be open later in the morning. I also noticed some wolf prints in the muddy places that dotted the ridgeline.

This part of the trail featured a couple views of Lake Desor but quickly fell into a woods walk. Indeed, virtually all of the Greenstone Ridge Trail west of Desor was a proverbial "walk in the woods." There are a number of hikers who disparage this section of the island's trail system. They see this walk as "boring" and "mundane." Yet, I have always enjoyed this part of the park. The alternately dense and open forest country, periodic climbs, and the isolation prevalent in this part of the park make the final third of the Greenstone a sound hiking experience. The land, and life in general, has many contours. We need to appreciate them all rather than snidely rating or judging each of them. This "boring" piece of trail has always struck me as peaceful and reflective in nature.

As I continued along the ridge the mosquitoes continued to dog me. It was difficult to stop for even a drink, as the bugs would immediately descend upon me if I quit moving. If I did stop to take a sip of liquid, the little monsters would dive bomb me and make every effort to get under my netting. Fortunately, as the day passed, I gained strength and broke into a better pace. As I sped up the bugs became less of a nuisance.

There is a feeling that can come over you when you hit your stride on the trail. Energy courses out to your limbs and you begin to eat up mileage. Coordination improves and your legs, arms, and trekking poles work as an efficient team. Your wind is solid and you carry on after an ascent only to find your breath returning to normal faster than at the start of the trip. Feeling fit on the trail is no mere act of Narcissism. It is the interaction of effort over time, tough terrain, and awareness.

When I reached the trail junction that spurred off toward Island Mine Campground I knew I was within a half-mile or so of the midpoint of today's hike. My water supply was low but I knew that I would reach a filtering point in about two miles. I headed on and continued to feel strong for the remainder of the hike.

From Island Mine on toward Windigo the terrain changed a bit. Leading up to that trail intersection there were periodic climbs and descents. After Island Mine, with very few exceptions, the terrain steadily headed downward. The Greenstone Ridge was withering away beneath my feet. All the hard won elevation I had gained along the way was melting in the face of long, bone-jarring descents. This downward slanting path persisted until just prior to the trail marker denoting my arrival at Windigo.

I have always found Windigo, and the western end of the island in general, to be more removed and appealing than other portions of the park. Far more people enter the park at Rock Harbor at the park's eastern end. The eastern park trails are generally more heavily traveled. Likewise, campgrounds located in the eastern half of the park tend to be more frequented. There are no housekeeping cabins, lodges, tractors pulling luggage racks, or restaurants at Windigo as there are at Rock Harbor. What you will find there is beautiful Washington Harbor, a lovely visitor center, a small general store where sandwiches & beverages can be purchased and eaten on a scenic patio overlooking the harbor, and kind & patient park staff. Rock Harbor is majestic and the people who work there are exceedingly helpful but, for me, "west is best" on Isle Royale.

In terms of today's wildlife encounters it was rather interesting. I saw several toads, one of which was the size of my fist. As I neared Windigo I startled a pair of foxes who were cavorting together and then scrambled off into the woods when they saw me. I ran into a third fox just before the trail marker denoting the boundary of Windigo. Then, as I headed down to the visitor center area after setting up in shelter number eight, I saw a cow moose feeding in Washington Harbor. It struck me as odd that I had solo hiked across the whole park only to see my first moose of the trip while I ambled down the path to shave and wash my hair.

Once I got to "downtown" Windigo I used the public bathroom to get cleaned up. It was so refreshing to shave and wash up after days on the trail. I felt and looked like a new man. The grizzled and greasy person who greeted me when I first looked in the mirror was replaced by me. In a day or so the cleanliness bloom would be off the rose once again after sweating and mud slogging, but sure felt good at the time.

After that cleansing experience I headed over to the visitor center. There I ran into Ranger Julie who had befriended my son Kyle and me over the past few seasons.

Julie had returned this season to Isle Royale after being a first grade teacher in New York City last year. I was glad to see her back at Isle Royale and working in a setting that she loved and felt at home in. It is important to know your place in the sun and try to appreciate it when you can. For Ranger Julie, Isle Royale was where she fit in and it was great to see her back in that setting.

After catching up with Ranger Julie I walked over to the general store. There I bought two turkey and cheese sandwiches, some chips, two pickles, and three cans of V-8 Juice. All of this stuff disappeared in short order. I also bought some pork & beans and canned corn to augment my dinner back in camp. All that I had left in my ration bag were two instant oatmeal packets which I planned to eat the next morning for breakfast before boarding the *Voyageur II* for a shuttle passage over to McCargoe Cove in the middle of the island's north side.

My original itinerary had me using the *Voyageur II* for two purposes. First, I had previously mailed my final three days provision to myself at Windigo via the *Voyageur II*. I planned to pick up this re-supply box when I boarded the boat tomorrow thus allowing me to set up my food bag on the ship. Included in that box were a couple food items such as juice boxes and pop-top ravioli that I could consume on the boat. In this way I could minimize the amount of food and trash that I had to bring along with me for the final few days of the trip.

The second use of the *Voyageur II* was one that many other hikers make use of as well. The *Voyageur II* circumnavigates the island on an every other day basis. On Monday, Wednesday, and Saturday the *Voyageur II* leaves Grand Portage. On those days it docks at Windigo and then circles the island's north shore en route to Rock Harbor where it stays overnight. The *Voyageur II* will drop passengers off at McCargoe Cove if prior arrangements have been made. Likewise, on Tuesday, Thursday, and Sunday after overnighting at Rock Harbor, the *Voyageur II* returns to Windigo via the island's south shore before heading back to Grand Portage. South shore shuttle stops can be scheduled for Daisy Farm, Chippewa Harbor, and Malone Bay. In this way the *Voyageur II* can assist a hiker interested in seeing certain portions of the island but who also has time or energy limitations.

Back at the Windigo visitor center I attended a mid-day presentation put on by Ranger Valerie. The topic was Isle Royale's moose population. Ranger Valerie, who I remember from prior years on the island, had returned to Isle Royale after a year absence wherein she worked at another park. Ranger Valerie did an excellent job of detailing features of moose physiognomy, behavior, and natural history. Ranger Valerie struck me as typical of the National Park Service staff that take on the educational and interpretive duties that exist in the park and do a fine job with those important tasks. If you happen to come out to Isle Royale and have the opportunity to go to a ranger led presentation or guided hike, by all means do so.

Back at the shelter it simply felt good to be on the shores of Washington Creek. Odd though it may sound, but I have always had a feeling of being home when I come to Windigo & Washington Creek. I cannot name another place on the island where I have felt more comfortable or at peace. It just feels comfortable to be at that quiet place where so many animals, birds, and other full time island inhabitants make their homes.

One feature of the Washington Creek Campground that is worth noting is its abundant wildlife. In a few hours a fortunate visitor can see red squirrels, gray jays, foxes, various woodpeckers, osprey, Merganser ducks, loons, cormorants, white pelicans, seagulls, river otters, bald eagles, and moose feeding in the creek or harbor.

This is a wonderful place to bring children for a low intensity visit to a wilderness park. Come out with your children, set up in a shelter for a couple days, watch for wildlife, look for wildflowers, take the nature hikes, walk the marked nature trail, day hike to Huginnin Cove, and share a beautiful place with your family.

As I sat outside my shelter writing these lines my attention was drawn to splashing in the creek. A Merganser mother was herding her babies along the far shore of the creek. The Merganser diligently hustled her clutch of young ones along and through the reeds. At one point she chided a straggler who came splashing back to the group. For ten minutes or so this family groups operated in front of me. Then off they went, down the creek and out of my sight.

Sometimes the best wildlife observations simply happen. You can tramp through the woods for days and encounter very few, if any, animals or interesting birds. Then, out of nowhere, something amazing can just happen. There is serendipity as well as order in the wild.

At the close of the day I went down to the visitor center to attend Ranger Julie's evening program on wolves. We had a chance to talk for a while and it was nice to get back in touch with a person who had been so kind to my son, my hiking partner Jack, and myself over the past four years. Julie's presentation was well attended and went very well. She was self-reportedly nervous as it was her first attempt with a new presentation but it was well received.

On the way back to camp I fell in step with Don from Milwaukee whom I had met at Todd Harbor and who had previously through-hiked the Appalachian Trail. We talked for a while and bid one another farewell. Don seemed like a very dedicated and strong hiker. He seemed like a man who could make his way in the wild and see good things from either the trail or the seat of a well-handled canoe.

In camp I spied a moose feeding further down the creek. After watching her feed from a distance I quietly walked over to the next-to-the-last shelter and observed her from about 30-40 feet away. As I stood along the shore behind a tree I saw the cow moose duck her head into the water, use its feet as a solid foundation, snort, drip water from its muzzle, chew, and shake itself dry like a floppy-eared dog. When I returned to my shelter I saw another cow feeding in the creek in the opposite direction. Washington Creek is a favorite dining spot for moose and these observations were a nice way to seal off a fine day. In fact, just before dark the sound of splashing in the creek caused me to jump out of my sleeping bag, slip on my boots, head outside, and watch another cow feed near the shelter, no more than twenty feet away as I stood near the picnic table. Every time I see a moose I find it just about as thrilling as the first time I did so.

Hiking Tips: (Note—Having completed the second of my three trail books, Lao Tzu's *Tao Te Ching*, this set of tips are drawn from that Taoist master's words.)
#28: "The difficult & the easy complement each other." – No backpacking trip will be without difficulty. In the wild things go wrong, equipment fails, bad weather lingers, and bugs can torment you like demons. Similarly, wondrous experiences can be had on the trail. The difficult and the easy, opposites though they may be, complement one another. Think back to a trip where you overcame adversity. That probably is a productive memory. Maintain that attitude and let it help you cope with the future hard knocks that the trail, and life, will hand out to you.

#29: "Let your wheels move along old ruts." –
Some people are driven to constantly see new things and
experience novelty. For others, the return to a familiar
place holds charm and comfort. It can feel good to revisit
a place and get to know it well. Trails look different when
hiked in opposite directions. The seasons change the visit.
By returning to a favorite place time and again one can
"move along old ruts" and thereby deepen our affection &
appreciation.

#30: "I hold firmly to stillness." – When you head
out to a place like Isle Royale you are afforded many
great opportunities. One is the gift of stillness. If you are
hiking alone you can choose to talk or not. On this
particular trip I went for days on the trail when I spoke
with no one. Similarly, while the woods are rarely still,
there is a peace that you can achieve by listening to them
in silence. Talking does not always enhance comm-
unication. Sometimes silence is the truest messenger of
them all. In the woods you can test this premise.

**#31: "One who excels in traveling leaves no wheel
tracks."** – The NPS has justly embraced a "Leave No
Trace" philosophy. If you visit Isle Royale, or any other
national park, leave things as they are. Take out what you
bring in & leave behind what is there. Your departure
should be like the mist as it glides away from the island.

**#32: "If you would take from a thing you must
first give to it."** – We live in a world where immediate
gratification is the desired norm. In the wild, a great deal
of effort is required to accomplish a positive result. A
distant place like Lake Desor must be hiked to on a
journey that can take one to five days depending upon a
variety of factors. A ridgeline view must first be ascended
before revealing itself to the traveler. If you go into the
wild expecting easy rewards you will be justly
disappointed. Each hiker must earn his or her benefits

through honest effort. From investing this effort comes the return.

#33: "Know when to stop, and you will meet with no danger." – There is no reward for pushing too hard, taking unnecessary risks on the trail, or exceeding your limits in the wilderness. Indeed, these actions carry great inherent risk if something goes wrong in a remote locale. If you want to enjoy Isle Royale do not go there to "push your limits" or set "personal bests" on the trail. Prepare and carry out your trip in a reasonable way so you can return home and to the park, healthy and whole.

#34: "The further one goes, the less one knows." – The return on a trip varies from person to person. However, in general, the more you rush the less you will see. Take your time and enjoy what is in front of you rather than worrying about mileage counts and the itinerary three days hence. If you are sitting on a creek bank and a Merganser mother swims out with ten ducklings that you wish to watch, so be it. Within reason, your schedule should be able to be adjusted to accommodate such an event. Do not push past the reason you came to Isle Royale in the first place.

#35: "A journey of a thousand miles begins with a single step." – Even the longest possible hike begins with the first step. If you reach a point in your trip, or during a day's hike, where you feel overwhelmed, take a break and get your perspective back. If you planned in a reasonable way and your health is good, you should be able to persevere and carry on to the finish. If not, adjust to new circumstances and modify your itinerary. In either case, every step you take is moving you toward your goal.

#36: "Not to know & to think that you know will lead to difficulty." - Being overconfident is a surefire pathway to disaster. I personally thought I knew Isle Royale very well. I had visited the park in June a number of times. My experience and judgment led me to believe solo hiking with a tarp rather than a tent would work out well. My over-confidence, linked to unreasonable weather and monster mosquito hatches, led to a disastrous experience. Avoid self-importance and overconfidence. Learn from such mistakes made by yourself and others and see the natural world with humility.

Day 6 (Wednesday—June 22): My sixth day on the island began with the sound of moose sloshing & snorting their way down the creek. It was too dark to see them, but moose activity around the area of my shelter was pronounced. One of the moose climbed right out of the creek and walked in front of the screened portion of the shelter. It issued a large snort as it passed perhaps as a form of moose greeting.

I slept in late and finally got up at about 7:30. A NPS work crew was just starting a re-roofing project on some of the nearby shelters. These young men and women were tearing off the old roof materials and hammering away. Given the youngsters' hard work I decided it was time to pack up and head down to Windigo where I would await the *Voyageur II*. Just prior to leaving camp I walked out to Washington Creek. Much to my surprise there was a moose cow grazing along the far shore. She appeared oblivious to both my presence and the racket that the workers were creating.

After watching the moose for 5-10 minutes I headed down to Windigo. At Windigo I purchased a couple V-8's and chatted with one of the maintenance workers. I then walked down to the visitor center and said goodbye to Rangers Valerie and Julie. I walked down to the dock where I spoke with a family from Bayfield, Wisconsin that had sailed into the harbor yesterday. Then, the *Voyageur II* sailed into view and arrived. I picked up my food re-supply box, stored away my grub, and settled into a comfortable seat.

Using the *Voyageur II* as a shuttle and re-supply vehicle is a grand idea. Once on board I was able to comfortably fill my food bag with new rations for the final three days of the trip. I also ate a lunch of canned ravioli and two juice boxes. My re-supply box and lunch debris were then deposited in the ship's garbage can. In this way I eliminated the need to carry any extra food weight all over the island. I also was able to have lunch on the boat with items I normally could not pack. Of course, it is always nice to be able to get rid of trash responsibly instead of having to carry it with you. I heartily recommend this re-supply method to hikers whose itinerary permits it to occur.

The cruise along the north shore of the island was most impressive. The coast on the north side of Isle Royale is rugged and rocky. In many ways it is similar to the New England coastline. Bays and rocky inlets dotted the shore. Trees stubbornly grew out of the rock shelf and hugged the coast. Beyond, glimpses of the Minong and Greenstone Ridges caught the sunlight. This land struck me as wild and picturesque. It was a place that could only be seen by way of Superior in order to appreciate it.

My original goal for today was to land at McCargoe Cove and hike the nine miles to Moskey Basin. However, as the day was beautiful, albeit warm, I toyed with the idea of hiking on through to Chippewa Harbor, about eleven miles from my docking point. Chippewa Harbor is a fine place with four shelters that sit on a bluff overlooking the small bay. The camp is set at the end of a four-mile spur trail that dead ends on the south shore. Going to Chippewa Harbor, which is often empty, would be a slightly longer day but a lovely spot indeed. I mulled these two options over as the boat approached my landing place and finally decided to let the day's circumstances dictate my final decision.

I got off the *Voyageur II* at McCargoe Cove and quickly hit the trail. It was about 2:00 and the sun was out and blazing. This was another hot day with inland temperatures seemingly at least in the mid-80's. As I hiked the three miles up toward West Chickenbone Campground I could feel the sweat begin to flow. Once again, the temperatures were unseasonably high and I felt their effects.

I passed a couple hikers near McCargoe and they were the only people I saw during the entire hike. As I walked on I kept an eye out for moose in Chickenbone Lake but saw none. Mid-day is among the worst times to see moose, and most other animals as well. This is particularly true in hot weather. However, I have seen numerous moose in ponds and lakes on warm days so the observations were worthwhile albeit futile.

Chickenbone Lake derives its name from its shape. The two arms of this wishbone shaped lake stretch out for a mile or so. There is a campground located roughly at the end of both of the lake's arms. West Chickenbone is a reasonable place to camp. The sites are on or near the lake. A beaver dam is nearby and these industrious creatures can be seen on the lake at work or in play mode. Moose frequent this area and are often seen in or near camp.

Conversely, East Chickenbone is a rather dismal campground. The sites are located up on a generally bare ridge out of sight of the lake. The camp's water source is far down a steep hill that makes it hard work to reach. On hot days there is little shade. In order to catch a look at the lake a camper has to trudge down the hill and through a wet area. In my own humble opinion, East Chickenbone is the least desirable campground in the park. I suggest staying there only if you have to or, perhaps, in fall when the temperatures abate & the insects are minimal.

After walking through West Chickenbone Camp I hiked up the generally steep trail that connected to the Greenstone Ridge. After reaching that intersection I headed on toward Lake Ritchie about three to four miles away. The hike toward Ritchie featured a couple elevation changes that got my heart pumping but was generally a moderate walk. The country along the way varied from open woods to a more scrub-like terrain. In general this was a pleasant walk that gradually descended toward Ritchie. Along the way I passed near some smaller lakes that are of interest to canoeists who portage through portions of this pathway.

I began to see Lake Ritchie through the trees and knew that the lakeside campground was about a mile further up the trail. The heat was beginning to really bother me, as often I had to wring out my headband and wipe my face. I could frequently see and feel sweat dripping from my nose. On rocky patches I could sense the heat radiating up from the trail as a sort of primeval microwave oven. I had really not expected such warm temperatures up north in June.

Lake Ritchie is a scenic backwoods lake. Several wooded islands dot its surface. The trail immediately leading up to it offers several overlooks of the lake. After a couple short but steep descents I arrived at the lake campground. A couple tents were set up but no one was out and about.

I paused for a few looks at the lake and surrounding area. When I paused I took several drinks of Gatorade and then pushed on. Just beyond Ritchie I came to the trail marker that pointed the way both to Chippewa Harbor and Moskey Basin. Given the heat, I did not have the desire to lengthen my day by over two additional miles. Chippewa Harbor is a lovely place that offers seclusion but the lure of Chippewa's picturesque scenery was insufficient to overpower the effects of a broiling day. All I wanted to do was get to camp and drop my pack in the shade. Thus, it was on to Moskey Basin.

The two miles on to Moskey Basin had three primary features. Sections of the trail traversed exposed rock with many wildflowers in view. Other portions of the route passed through scrub forest. Finally, some stretches went through conifer woods with moderate sized trees. This was a pleasant forty-minute walk and ended for me at the heavenly trail marker that led me down to Moskey Basin.

If you ask repeat visitors to this park what some of their favorite scenic spots on the island are it is probable that Moskey Basin will make their list. The campground is located at the end of Rock Harbor where it narrows down and finally peters out. The campsites and shelters are along a small dead end finger bay. If you can get a shelter your front yard will be sloping stone that drops down to the bay. Across the small bay you will see other sloping shores of stone that are hundreds of millions of years old. To the east Rock Harbor stretches out into Lake Superior. On many days you can see fog rolling along the harbor. The cold waters of this mighty lake chill the heat of the inland trail.

It felt good to unload my pack and stretch out in a comfortable shelter. I cooked dinner, set my clothes out to dry on the ageless rocks, and felt my body tingling from the fatigue of the trail. It is a fine feeling to know that your body has worked hard in pursuit of a worthy goal. At Moskey Basin I was tired but also aware that a certain amount of work was required of me to get there. The rewards for this labor was time in a cozy spot, being part of a wondrous setting, and my body's messages to rest after a hot day on the trail.

As the day closed I lay in my sleeping bag reading *Zen Lessons,* my final pack book. Periodically, I stared at the two small candles I lit to read by. Set against the reddish-brown wood of the shelter wall, these tiny flames gave off a warm feeling. Their light reflected against the wooden wall and set off its glowing finish. There is something calming about a candle set out to stare at. The flickering light is both calming and functional. The two flames struck me as small islands of light in a sea of darkness. I lay there and pondered what I had done to deserve such a relaxing way to close another good day in this fine place.

Hiking Tips:

#37: Think About Hydration – Hiking is a demanding endeavor. I have been involved in cross country cycling, jogging, hockey, and other forms of exercise. None of these activities is as entirely demanding as backpacking. Therefore, be aware of the need to hydrate. As you walk along with a significant burden on your back, you will lose fluids at a rapid rate. On hot days this reality becomes critical. Be sure to carry enough fluids with you. Stop at filtering points and drink before replenishing your water. Take water breaks when you need them and at least once every hour. After reaching camp be sure to drink throughout the evening in order to rehydrate yourself. At Isle Royale many of the trails abut Lake Superior or come near inland lakes & streams. However, the ridge trails have very limited water sources between camps. Keep that fact in mind and hydrate adequately.

#38: Bring Plenty of Moleskin – Isle Royale's trails can punish your feet. Nothing can dampen a hike more than foot problems. Come prepared for blisters. Moleskin, band-aids, and related items are a must in your first aid kit. Do not scrimp on bringing these foot savers along with you. Their availability may salvage an otherwise doomed hike.

#39: Carry Spare Hiking Socks & Liners – Yes, keeping your pack weight down is vital. However, it is your feet that take the greatest pounding on the trail. Therefore, carry extra socks and liners. Also, if you have not already done so, use lightweight & wicking liners under your heavy duty hiking socks. The liners reduce foot friction & go a long way toward eliminating blisters. Further, use outer socks that have adequate heel, toe, and sole padding and that are quick drying. Having socks that are wet lumps refusing to dry will not help you enjoy Isle Royale or any other hiking venue.

#40: Use Gatorade or Some Other Powdered Enhancement – Over the years I have made it a habit to pack powdered Gatorade in my food bag. Every hiking day I mix a liter of Gatorade & drink it along the trail. I have found that Gatorade provides me with energy and relief from emerging fatigue symptoms. If you do not like Gatorade there are other powdered sports drinks or electrolyte enhancers available. This sort of energy boost and replenishment should not be underestimated.

#41: Watch for Moose at Windigo – Many people come to Isle Royale specifically to see moose. While there are several places where moose can regularly be seen such as Chickenbone Lake, McCargoe Cove, Hidden Lake, and Feldtmann Lake, my own experience leads me to believe that Washington Creek & Harbor are excellent spots for moose watching. On this particular trip I hiked the length of the island and saw no moose. In one day at Windigo, I saw six. There are no guarantees that going to Windigo will result in moose descending on your campsite for your viewing pleasure. But, it is a reasonable bet that you stand a good chance of seeing one if you sit quietly in front of a shelter along the creek and just watch and listen.

#42: Think About Using the *Voyageur II* for Re-Supply – As mentioned previously, you can send a re-supply box to yourself via the *Voyageur II*. In order to accomplish this feat you need to ship the box via US Mail to yourself C/O the *Voyageur II* in Grand Portage, MN 55605. In the lower left hand corner of the box place the date & location where you will pick up the box. Be sure it is a site where the boat regularly plans on stopping on your designated delivery date. Generally, Rock Harbor and Windigo are the recommended destinations to mail your re-supply box. Send out your box, or have some one else do so, about a week or so ahead of you designated pick up date. Be on the dock at the appointed time. This is a fine way to supply yourself & your party on an extended trip. In this manner you can avoid having to carry excess food weight and the cost of "hit or miss" food purchases at the camp stores at either end of the park.

#43: Rest at Day's End – Once you have established camp—and chores are done—rest. For some people there is a tendency to hustle around from here to there in camp with no time set aside for rest & recharging. Remember—getting where you are camped was not easy. Lie down in your tent or shelter and let your body and mind relax. There will be time later for exploration if you so desire. It stays light a long time on a clear summer or spring evening in the Northland. Through rest you allow tired joints, muscles, and feet to decompress and recover. Resting is part of effective backpacking. If you do not establish time to rest after a hard day on the trail, your body will pay a price. On lengthy hikes schedule a rest day in every week or expect an eventual physical problem.

Day 7 (Thursday—June 23): I awoke this morning to the crashing sounds of a thunderstorm. Lightening flashes brightened the dim early morning sky. Rain heavily fell as the skies let loose with a downpour. It was as if the pent up humidity of the past few days had finally reached the saturation point and now had to thoroughly drench the land.

Faced with this development I decided to sleep in and get a later start than usual. My feet felt a bit sore and I was generally more tired than usual at this stage of a hike due to the continuous hot weather. If this had been a longer trip I would have considered taking today as a rest day while recuperating by the shores of Moskey Basin. Instead, I decided to have an abbreviated hiking day and simply head over to Daisy Farm just four miles up the Rock Harbor Trail. Tomorrow I planned on climbing up to Mount Ojibway before walking along the Greenstone toward Tobin Harbor and my trip's endpoint. As the rain continued to fall I felt comfortable with that decision. Even if the showers persisted all day, I would be able to dry out at Daisy Farm.

Last night I finished my final pack book—*Zen Lessons: The Art of Leadership.* This compilation of Zen writings from 12th century Chinese masters was uneven in quality but did have some appropriate lessons for this journey and beyond. I spent some time taking in these ancient leadership lessons and applied them to a wilderness excursion. In writing the following points I came to understand that to lead we must follow the paths that are before us in much the same way that a backpacker takes the trail for what it is. Listed below are a few of these lessons and their applications to Isle Royale and other wilderness domains beyond.

- **"There are three essentials to leadership: humanity, clarity, & courage."** – If you wish to succeed in the wild, you must understand its value, know why you have entered it, and have the strength to endure its challenges.
- **"Errant conceptions and emotional thinking all melt in the real mind."** – The woods are a place to let go of the mental clutter that fills all too much of our lives. In the wild, life is simplified. You think about distances, terrain, weather, water, food, and the rhythm of the day. Your "real mind" is focused on the basics of life & what surrounds you and not the phantasmagoria of fears that crowd us into corners in day-to-day life.
- **"It is left to nature whether one may experience calamity or disasters, gain or loss."** – In the wilderness you give up control of many things. Regardless of your wishes, rain, heat, and wind will come. Your hopes cannot change the steep hill or span the wet portions of the trail. The world is what it is, and all we can do is acknowledge that reality & prepare as best we can.
- **"What has long been neglected cannot be restored immediately."** – If you have not adequately planned your trip, looked after your gear, or conditioned yourself then your trip will be difficult. Over time you can recover, but it will not happen over night & it will be difficult.
- **"People who aggrandize themselves are harmful to others."** – When you speak with other hikers refrain from glorifying what you have seen or done. Ask questions and listen rather than boasting about all the miles you have covered, how far you can go in a day, or how many moose you have seen. Be pleasant and helpful or simply courteous. No one

wants to meet a braggart who sees only their own needs and not those of other people.

- **"A beautiful accomplishment takes a long time, ultimately involving lifelong consideration."** – If you are a parent or have loved someone you know the truth of this declaration. No one can truly know Isle Royale or any natural setting. Life is simply too complicated for that. But, with patience, diligence, effort, and time you can learn about a place or a relationship. In that process you can also discover a great deal about yourself as well.
- **"Therefore a supervisor is one who when safe does not forget danger, and who in times of order does not forget about disorder."** – As the Boy Scouts say—"Be Prepared!" When things are taken for granted, discord follows. This fact is true in life, love, relationships, and certainly on the trail & in camp. Do not become either paranoid or complacent. Reduce your anxiety by being thoughtful and ready. A less anxious mind is one that is more observant and luckier.
- **"If you cannot decide for yourself beforehand, you should ask experienced elders about it."** – If you have questions about visiting Isle Royale, or about backpacking in general, ask them to reputable folks. Keep those important questions in mind and go to an outfitter store, read & research, use the Internet, call the park, or join a hiking or environmental organization. There are people out there who have the answer to your questions. Do not be afraid to ask them, as there are few foolish questions from earnest inquirers.

At the close of this Zen book I came across a poem that struck a chord of memory with me. The Zen master

Jiantong had written the poem centuries ago while he lived in seclusion on Mount Guon in Fanzang, China. In many ways the poem captured the essence of being in the wild & all the joys therein:

The Hearths without fire, the
knapsack empty,
The snow is like apricot blossoms,
falling at year's end.
Patched robe over my head, burning
scraps of wood,
I am not conscious of my
body in peaceful quietude
In daily life I go on the Way
by myself,
Not rushing after glory & fame

Centuries ago a Chinese teacher wrote these words. Today, for many wilderness travelers, the journey is the same. To find external wonder and inner peace in the natural order without thought of fame or glory. Is that not reason enough to don a pack or take a beloved child's hand and walk along a woodland path?

In terms of today's hike, as one hiker I passed rightfully commented, "I should have brought my canoe." The morning thunderstorm had flooded much of the trail system. Significant parts of the trail resembled a running stream more than a footpath. In other places, small ponds had replaced the trail. No matter how carefully I tried to negotiate the wet portions of the trail I ended up with wet feet. Today's hike was short but a real boot-soaker.

The four miles from Moskey to Daisy Farm was a fine hike. Sections of the trail had me scrambling up, over, and onto parts of the Canadian Shield. These rocky portions of the trail were hard on my feet but pleasing to the eye. In some places entire rocky hillsides were covered with predominantly yellow wildflowers. However, on a wet day the rocky walking was not only scenic—but also treacherous.

When walking on rocks that are wet you need to slow down and take extra precautions. On two occasions today I ended up slipping. Once I fell but managed to land on my pack so no damage was done. The second time I caught my balance but did so by planting my right foot in a shin deep pool of rainwater. On Isle Royale there are many rocky trails and a great deal of water. Be careful and watch your step.

I passed a few hikers on the way to Daisy Farm. Each of them seemed a bit discouraged by the trail conditions. While sometimes a long face is understandable, you do have to go with the flow when hiking. You have absolutely no control over important factors such as weather, trail conditions, or water sources. All you can do is prepare in advance for contingencies, accept what comes, and make the best of things.

I reached camp by early afternoon after taking my time getting started from Moskey Basin. My clothing was drenched both from water and the effort of getting to Daisy Farm. The four miles between Daisy and Moskey should not be underestimated. Those miles are harder than long stretches of either the Greenstone or Feldtmann Ridge Trails.

Having entered camp I was surprised by how flooded it was. The feeder trail that runs by the lake and in front of many of the shelters was covered in deep water. The areas in front of most of the shelters were also flooded. So I waded my way up to an empty shelter, stripped off my sodden clothing & boots, emptied my pack, and filtered water.

It was good to be in camp after essentially a short-range change in my base of operations. I needed a rest day and after a short hike I essentially had one. The hike to

Daisy stretched out & broke in my legs while also giving me a sense of having earned my meals for the day. While in camp I also noticed that it was clouding up once again and rain looked to be in the offing. Given that reality it felt doubly good to be in camp rather than hiking on up the greenstone in the face of further thunderstorms. I have hiked through thunderstorms on Isle Royale's ridgelines and, while those were interesting experiences, they were not ones I really wished to repeat in the near future.

Hiking Tips:

#44: Slow your Pace on Wet Trails – If trail conditions are wet, there is no good return on speedy walking. You will need to slow you pace and plan out many of your footsteps. Hiking in wet areas can be like solving a puzzle. You may find yourself plotting out your path while mentally saying, "Let's see—I'll stay to the left & go rock, to stone, to root, and then over the far edge of the pond." You cannot rush this process while steadying your patience. If you hurry you will be either lucky or drenched.

#45: Be Careful on Wet Rocks – This point is worthy of being doubly made. Isle Royale is a rocky place. Mornings can be dewy. It rains on an unpredictable schedule. Even on dry days your boots may well be soaked from crossing wet areas or due to groundcover moisture. On wet rocks slow down, plant your feet & hiking poles carefully, attend to each step, and be ready for slips. On ascents try to find irregularities or notches in the rocks to enhance your boot's grip. On descents be extremely careful as a fall can be much more dangerous. Shorten your stride and read the terrain for the safest pathway. If you can avoid rock and step on more secure parts of the trail, do so. If the rock face slants sharply try to stay near the bottom so that you can catch your balance on the nearby ground rather than tumbling down the rock. If there are stairway-like elements to the trail use them but check your footing with each step. Do not try to be macho and leap up the rock stairs two at a time like you might do at home. Enjoy the rocky vistas and Spartan terrain but do so while being cautious. It is a long way between ranger stations and some trails are sparsely traveled. The backcountry is not a place to injure yourself so take your time while being watchful.

#46: Cover Up in Camp – Once you have established camp you will want to change into dry clothes. Your camp clothes should be lightweight, quick drying, and designed to provide cover from biting insects. When you are hiking you are a moving target for biting pests. On the move you can push through particularly nasty buggy areas. In camp, you are like the proverbial fish in a barrel with the bugs as the marksmen. That is why long pants and a long sleeved shirt or windbreaker are recommended camp clothing. You have worked hard to get to your campsite. Do you really want to spend all your camp time hunkered down in your tent, bivy, or shelter if you do not have to? Wear protective clothing and you will be much freer to spend time out and about in camp.

#47: Hike in Shorts – This is a debatable point as many people would rather cover up their legs while hiking in order to protect themselves from insects, sticks, and poisonous plant growth. However, my own experience has taught me to believe in the advantages of hiking in quick drying shorts. In shorts I feel much cooler and have far greater freedom of movement. Dews and damps quickly soak long pants. Legs dry easier than fabric. Further, shorts help you r body's natural cooling system based upon perspiration and evaporation work more completely. You can spray your legs with bug dope and have a cooler time on the trail if you go with reasonable hiking shorts.

#48: Bring Enough Bug Spray – Obnoxious though it may be to spray chemicals on your skin and clothes, in bug season you really have very few other options if you wish to remain sane. Without the right clothes and adequate bug spray, insects can literally destroy a hiking trip. On the trail if you are without insect repellent you will be hard pressed to even take a water break. In camp, you will be a prisoner in your tent. Always bring more bug spray than you think is necessary. Those few extra ounces may be the salvation of your entire trip.

#49: Try to Think Like an Animal – If you are interested in observing wildlife then you need to know at least a little bit about animal behavior. For example, moose hate heat. When the temperature rises above 45-50 degrees you will probably not see them ranging about on exposed ridges or in sunny meadows. During those types of days pause and survey beaver ponds and lakes for browsing moose. Likewise, look for foxes in camps in the evening or patrolling trails in the morning. If you try to think like the animals you want to see you increase your chances of observing them. Certainly, chance encounters with wildlife happen all the time. But over time, you will see more if you take the time to learn about wildlife and the rhymes & reasons of their lives.

Day 8 (Tuesday—June 24): For the first time this trip I had difficulty sleeping last night. A few work-related dreams that would classify as nightmares awoke me throughout the night. Rarely have I dreamed of such matters on Isle Royale, so I think my mind is telling me something important. When your instincts speak to you it is important to listen to their messages. Isle Royale had

61

always been a place of clarity to me. Coming to the park had become an annual ritual or even a pilgrimage. Waking up in the middle of the night afraid of vocational phantoms was prescriptive. These sorts of mental dial tones have to be acknowledged and answered. Once again, the Northwoods had spoken to me and helped me at least realize how deep some of my feelings, anxieties, and problems were.

The morning of my final hiking day of this trip was clear. Much of the run-off from yesterday's big storm had disappeared from camp. Of course, despite the absence of much of the obvious standing water, the trails would still be soaked. However, I did not anticipate seeing the veritable streams that I had encountered the prior day heading into Daisy from Moskey Basin.

Today's agenda had the potential for a grand hike. First I would climb up to Mount Ojibway. Then, after reaching the observation tower and taking a look at the scenery form its top, I would follow the Greenstone over to Mount Franklin. From there I would descend to the Tobin Harbor Trail and hike along it until I reached Rock Harbor. The total distance for the day would be nine miles and the scenery had always been among my favorite in the park.

I broke camp and hit the trail at 6:30 in the morning. Daisy Farm was quiet as most of the folks staying there were sleeping in. Almost immediately the trail began to climb. The hike up to Mount Ojibway along the Greenstone Ridge is about 1.7 miles. At first a hiker climbs a fairly steep hill just outside of Daisy Farm. Then the trail drops down to a boardwalk area near a beaver dam. After crossing that wet area you begin a series of climbs that eventually get you to Mount Ojibway.

Writing about this trail as I did in the last paragraph is one thing—hiking it is another. Generally, if you start early you will see few, if any, other hikers. As the sun rises in the east, the morning light makes this rugged stretch of trail seem even more remote. While you walk, if you look around, you can get a sense of the toughness of Isle Royale's terrain.

As you descend toward the wet area down in the valley you will catch a look at the fire tower up on the ridge. At that point the tower appears quite near. But, in reality, there is a hard mile remaining until reaching that destination. During that mile a hiker will have both head - on and switchback climbs. Portions of the trail are rocky and, on this day, were very slick due to moisture. At two places a backpacker can easily think he or she is finished climbing, but these are false summits. Finally, as the tower came into view a second time I knew I was within a quarter mile or so of the ridge.

Once I reached the tower I dropped my pack, drank some Gatorade, and headed up the tower. The Mount Ojibway Tower is used to assist in taking atmospheric readings. This is a five-story structure of which visitors can climb four in order to secure a panoramic view of the eastern end of the island. The view from Mount Ojibway is striking. To the south you can see the Rock Harbor Lighthouse, Mott Island, Rock Harbor, the outer islands, and vast Lake Superior beyond. To the north Canada & its outer islands loom as well as portions of Isle Royale's Amygdaloid Island. To the west viewers can observe several of the inland lakes inclusive of Chickenbone, Hatchet, & Ritchie along with a glimpse of McCargoe Cove. Finally, to the east, Isle Royale appears to come to an arrowhead point with the land gently elevating toward Mount Franklin. This spot may not be the best view in the park but I am hard pressed to think of a better one.

After coming off the tower I headed east along the Greenstone Ridge. Like many hikers I know who have taken this walk, I was anxious to get into what I knew from past experience would be a very scenic walk. In my hurry to get going I missed the start of the trail going east. I backtracked a hundred yards or so and found my way. If you hike this way be careful to locate the Greenstone heading east. The start of the trail from the tower is a tad obscure so watch your directions and keep an eye pealed for the rock cairns that have been placed as trail markers along the rocky patches.

The walk from Mount Ojibway to Mount Franklin was simply first rate. There were some moderate climbs and descents but generally the terrain was fairly level. There were many big views of both the north and south sides of the island. Wildflowers of many colors dotted the landscape as I walked along this piece of ground. Trees varied from evergreens to deciduous and provided a variation that was unusual to walk through. All in all, this section of the Greenstone stood out as particularly appealing.

The day was beautiful but still fairly humid. My clothing was wringing wet well before I made the short climb up to Mount Franklin. In fact temperatures throughout this trip were unseasonably oppressive. The weather, albeit dry save for the big thunderstorm of the other day, was much more like late July or August back in Illinois rather than a June hiking trip on Isle Royale. If I could have predicted these conditions I would have left a couple pounds of cold weather clothing back home. But, as is the norm in this park, weather conditions were unpredictable. So, preparing for sudden shifts in temperature and precipitation is always advisable if you are considering a visit to Isle Royale.

At Mount Franklin I dropped my pack, emptied one of my water bottles, wrung out my headband, and sat down among the rocks by the overlook. The wind was blowing hard and it felt great to be cooled by it. Looking down at my legs & shorts, I could see just how saturated my clothing was. I felt grand but hiking in such hot weather more than doubles the impact of the trail upon your body. Resting at Mount Franklin for a bit was in order and so, I did.

The overlook at Mount Franklin offers hikers an outstanding view. Directly in front of me, down by the south shore, sat Lane Cove. Beyond the cove were some islands and rocky points. Across mighty Superior was Canada with Pie Island dominating the horizon. Every time I pass this way I sit in this spot for a while and reflect on many things.

Life is such a short journey. We spend so much of it worrying about problems, children's welfare, relationships, money, and ego. Before you know it, life passes you by. Sitting among the rocks at Mount Franklin, gazing out at nature's grandeur, and easing my worn body, life became much simpler for me. Our place in the world as individuals is unique. But we are part of a greater whole. All around us life moves on with us as just one tiny part of it. It is in our own mind's eye that we confuse transitory wants & needs with importance. On Mount Franklin, it was possible for me to see the interconnectedness of all life. That spirit can be carried along to other parts of daily life. Therein lie both the challenge and the opportunity created by a trip such as this one.

After resting for a while I hefted my pack and headed on down the trail. About two tenths of a mile east rests the intersection with the 2.4 mile long Lane Cove Trail. If you take that walk you will descend a series of steep switchbacks and walk down into scrub country where there was once prominent beaver activity. Lane Cove is a lovely north shore camp with no shelters and a handful of tent sites. The camp sits at the end of this dead end trail and, although very buggy at times, it is a fine place to stay. Indeed, some veteran hikers in the park describe the Lane Cove area as perhaps the best opportunity a backpacker has of attaining a true wilderness feel in the more heavily used eastern end of the park.

Today I passed on the opportunity of going to Lane Cove and instead started to head down the adjoining trail heading toward Tobin Harbor. For about 1.5 miles the trail dropped almost continuously. Some of the descents wound their way through wooded areas. These portions of the trail were typically wet with many exposed rocks and roots. Other parts of the trail took me down rocky patches that were exceedingly slippery. I adjusted my pace and made it down without any incidents or spills.

Near the intersection with the Tobin Harbor Trail I came across a large beaver pond. In the past I had often seen moose browsing in this spot. On this day no moose were present. Once again I have not seen a single moose on the trail. The combination of a significant winter die off and the hot weather has made it extra hard to catch a glimpse of Isle Royale's moose population. I was grateful for my moose sightings at Windigo but it was surprising to see no others as I had walked all across the island and back.

Shortly after passing the aforementioned beaver pond the trail traversed a large downhill section of rock. Several switchbacks meandered among the wildflowers and took me downhill. Just after this descent I came to the Tobin Harbor Trail intersection. At this point a hiker can continue east for three miles to Rock Harbor or take a short spur trail up and over a hill to Three Mile Camp. I chose to continue on along the Tobin Harbor Trail toward my trip endpoint.

The Tobin Harbor Trail roughly parallels the Rock Harbor Trail leading up to Rock Harbor. Both trails arrive at the same location but they are very different in nature. The Rock Harbor Trail is very scenic but also full of rocks and roots making it a harder than anticipated walk. Conversely, the walk along Tobin Harbor is pretty but much more level. There are three or four hills along Tobin Harbor but none of them are terribly taxing thus making it an easier path to take toward Rock Harbor.

Along Tobin Harbor I saw Mergansers, cormorants, & loons. At one point I was listening to the north wind rush through the trees a loon began to call from the harbor. I stopped and listened to these woodland sounds and noticed that I was smiling. Nearby song sparrows elicited their charming calls. The azure sky opened up above me into infinity. Tobin Harbor reflected this blue atmospheric canopy and stood out in its blueness. Standing there—seeing & hearing those things—life was good.

I pushed up onto Rock Harbor & passed a Boy Scout group from Milford, Michigan. They were taking a break and we chatted for a bit. The boys and their leaders had seen a moose & calf in camp the previous night. In fact, according to one of the lads, "The moose almost tromped on our tent!" The group had matching shirts with a drawing of Isle Royale on the back. It was nice to see kids and adults having a good time together in the woods. Through direct experience people learn and develop their ethical core. It is a fine thing to introduce children to nature and hope that a love of it speaks to them in a voice that is understood.

About a half hour after passing the scouts I arrived at Rock Harbor. Reaching Rock Harbor at the end of a hike is always a bittersweet moment for me. On the plus side, this arrival signified the safe completion of another trip to the park. Dropping my pack in a shelter and completing camp chores for a final time this trip was a relief. Rock Harbor has a café & restaurant where food other than dehydrated meals could be found. The sunny harbor is a place to relax and unwind after the effort of a long hike.

On the other hand, it can be jarring to arrive back in the embrace of "civilization". With its lodge and housekeeping cabins, Rock Harbor caters to a clientele far different than either the backcountry or Windigo. Small tractors shuttle from the dock to the various accommodations carrying guest's luggage. People walk about who are clean and dressed as tourists rather than grimy backpackers. It was almost as if I had walked into a completely different world. Sometimes this transition has unnerved me as the modern world rushes in a little too swiftly.

Rock Harbor does offer some interesting features. Boat tours can be booked that feature guided hikes at places such as Lookout Louise, the mines at McCargoe Cove, Passage Island, and other locations. A somewhat pricey but convenient water taxi service can be chartered to drop you or pick you up at several points in the east end of the park. Evening programs are also a regular feature as well. As previously noted, there are two places to eat inclusive of the lodge restaurant and a small adjoining café. Comfortable lodging can be secured as well but the prices are a tad steep. The Seaplane from Hancock lands at Rock Harbor as well as Windigo thus offering a quick shuttle service either back to the mainland or to the far end of the park. Canoes, motorboats, and kayaks can be rented for time periods ranging from a few hours to multiple weeks. Taken as a whole, you can do things at Rock Harbor that are unavailable anywhere else in the park.

A visitor to Rock Harbor can also take the scenic Stoll Trail. This figure eight trail can be taken as a 1.5-3 mile hike. While there are some rocky stretches and a few moderate hills, the Stoll Trail is a relatively easy walk. If you go all the way out to the far point, you will experience one of the best views in the park. At Scoville Point you will be able to sit on rocky bluffs fifty feet above Lake Superior. Your view will include the end of the Greenstone Ridge as it slips into Superior, rocky outer islands, crashing waves, tidal pools, and a general sense of being in the presence of a majestic place. If you spend some time at Scoville Point you will have a sense of the vastness and power of Lake Superior.

For me, one of the rituals of reaching Rock Harbor is to go to the café and have a meal. I generally sit down with a quart jug of milk purchased at the nearby camp store across the way from the visitor center. Then I eat a meal that seems grand after a steady diet of pack food. I followed this routine on this occasion and thoroughly enjoyed my indulgence. Lunch was then augmented with two forty-seven cent ice cream sandwiches from the store that I ate while basking in the warm sun at a picnic table facing the harbor. While sitting there I chatted with a fisherman from Iron Mountain, Michigan who had been coming to the park for the past sixteen years. This gentleman has the *Ranger III* transport his fishing boat over with him for a charge of $160. He then spends a couple weeks pursuing lake trout and other deep-water quarry. What a nice guy and yet another example of the quality of folks who visit this hard to reach place time and again.

Much of the afternoon was spent at Rock Harbor writing and quietly sitting by the lake. I did strike up another long and hearty conversation with Dave, the aforementioned fisherman from Iron Mountain. We traded stories about Isle Royale and our mutual love of this place. What was interesting was that Dave's perspective, as a deep seas fisherman, was similar to my own as a backpacker. Dave spoke of Belle Island, Crystal Cove, Caribou Island, and Blake's Point, each of which was someplace that I, as a hiker, had never been. Likewise, I spoke of inland lakes and trails that were accessible to foot sloggers and not boaters. Yet, despite this fundamental difference, we shared a common need to return to this park and revisit favorite places.

During our talk Dave shared one personal story that I believe sums up the love and draw that repeat visitors to Isle Royale have for this place. Over the years Dave and his wife have generally come here to fish together. Over the past few years responsibilities as a grandmother have kept Dave's wife from accompanying him. The couple's preferred time to come out to Isle Royale was mid-June where they would combine a fishing trip with the June 15th celebration of their wedding anniversary. For the past few years Dave's wife has sent him off at the appointed time, despite it overlapping with their wedding anniversary. Her sole instruction was that at 6:00 PM central time, not the crazy island time, Dave would raise a glass in toast to the south. Dave's wife pledged to do the same, at the same hour, with her glass raised to the north. Such is the dedication and love that can be born of this distant & compelling place.

Hiking Tips:

#50: Watch for Cairns – On Isle Royale there are no trail markers or blazes on the trees. Occasionally, along the ridgelines, there is some marking but that is extremely rare. In some places where the trail crosses bare rock, cairns are provided to guide you. If you are not aware of what a cairn is, and there is no shame in not knowing what this rarely used word means, it simply refers to a small pile of rocks used as a marker. The word comes from old Gaelic, and has been translated by some to mean "marker or place of death." Hopefully that old definition will have no significance for you other than to make you more aware of the need to pay attention for cairns as you hike. On trails like the Greenstone, Minong, Feldtmann, and Rock Harbor cairns can be very important. On the Minong, in particular, parts of the trail can be very obscure. Use the cairns as guideposts and do not be embarrassed to occasionally backtrack in order to retrace your way.

#51: Use Dehydrated Foods – This is essentially a matter of preference but food equals both potential energy and bulk weight in your pack. You can only comfortably fit so many items into your pack. Dehydrated foodstuffs are an excellent way of maximizing energy production while minimizing pack weight. For example, a package of tuna will provided you with a certain number of calories and will weigh about seven ounces. A dehydrated rice and chicken meal for one will give you about 400 calories, produces thirteen ounces of food after preparation, and weighs just three to four ounces. Dried fruit provides needed vitamins and can easily be carried. Fresh fruit is prohibitively heavy, may introduce non-native trees if not properly disposed of, and will spoil on the trail. Given the logistical limitations inherent in backpacking, dehydrated foods are the way to go.

#52: Pack Some Candles for Evening – If you are staying in a shelter the small flame from a hiker's candle is a pleasant way to read or write after dark. Also, if traveling with a significant other, candlelight can be very romantic. There is a charm to a candle's fluttering flame that you will appreciate out in the backcountry whether you are alone or with someone you care about. Of course, always be careful to douse your candle before falling asleep, which is doubly important if you are very tired at the end of a taxing day.

#53: Do not Plan on Campfires – You can, indeed, have a campfire at some of Isle Royale's campgrounds. However, fires are only permitted at campgrounds where a metal fire ring or grill is provided. Camps with such arrangements include Siskiwit Bay, Todd Harbor, McCargoe Cove, Chippewa Harbor, and Little Todd Harbor. While I have had a few campfires on Isle Royale it is a hit or miss prospect. The day you arrive at a campground with a fire ring or grill it may be raining or soaked from prior rains. Finding downed wood that is dry & not green can be a chore. You probably will be tired from miles of hiking and having to tromp around off trail in search of firewood may be one too many tasks for the day. Therefore, do not be disappointed if you leave Isle Royale without too many, if any, campfire experiences. Also, if you find a stone fire ring, do not use it as it is an artificial creation of past campers and not a ranger sanctioned campfire spot.

#54: Wear Solid Footgear – Isle Royale is not the place to break in new boots. Wear solid footgear that you are comfortable backpacking in. The rocks, roots, climbs, and descents that are prominent features of the park's trail system will punish you if your footwear is inadequate. Whether you favor full boots or low-cuts is a personal choice. What is important is that your boots are durable, offer adequate protection, support you & your pack weight, and are a proven commodity.

#55: Bring a Lightweight Camera – Photos generally never do justice to a picturesque place like Isle Royale. However, a few pictures of wildlife, vistas, overlooks, or lakes can be a nice keepsake of your trip. Photos can also help illustrate your experiences for those loved ones or acquaintances left behind. No one can really understand your trip the way you do but your pictures can be the catalyst for conversation and curiosity.

#56: Share Helpful Advice When Possible – If you have experience backpacking, and have visited the park on prior occasions, you may be able to help people you encounter along the trail or in camp who appear puzzled. Issues related to upcoming terrain, water sources, campground choices, or trip options may come up in conversation with such folks. If you can offer meaningful & helpful advice and the opportunity presents itself, do so. Whether your counsel is heeded or not is the decision of others, but at least you have made a goodhearted offer.

#57: Bring a Reliable Water Filter – Superior is a deep and relatively pure lake but you should not assume that its water is potable. Isle Royale's inland lakes contain the possibility of protozoan induced infections such as Giardia. In addition, unfiltered water may contain tapeworm eggs that you would do well to avoid. Therefore, it is essential to have a dependable water filter that can block impurities as small as three microns in size. You can certainly boil water to purify it but that process is an impractical option. Boiling to purify requires bringing your water to a rolling boil for five minutes. Given the amount of water needed to keep an active backpacker hydrated and to cook meals with, you will run out of stove fuel without satisfying those requirements. Bring a workmanlike filter and know how to use and repair it in the field.

#58: Think creatively with your Itinerary – Getting to Isle Royale is complex and requires careful planning. However, given the number of transport options available, you can schedule a trip that takes you to places far removed from one another. Do you want to see Malone Bay but resist the idea of backtracking up the seven-mile dead end trail that takes you there from the greenstone Ridge at the Ishpeming tower? If so the arrange to catch the *Voyageur II* at Malone Bay and shuttle over to Windigo and continue your hike from there. Are you interested in starting your Greenstone Ridge hike at its eastern terminus up at Lookout Louise? Then make use of the Rock Harbor boat tour & guided hike up to that spot that takes place on a weekly basis and set out down the ridge from there. There are a number of creative options that can be part of your itinerary if you take the time to ask questions, research possibilities, and plan ahead.

#59: If Solo Hiking let Caution be your Byword – A solo hiker has great opportunities for solitude. There are many advantages and great independence inherent in hiking alone. Still, there is also greater responsibility wrapped up in hiking alone. If you hike alone you need to be doubly cautious and aware of risks. The solo hiker needs to self-monitor water intake, energy levels, break times, and ambition. He or she must also fully realize that any sort of injury has much greater ramifications when you are alone. Hiking alone can be an amazing experience but it is one for a thoughtful and focused traveler.

Day 9 (Wednesday—June 25): Departures from Isle Royale are always very emotional for me. A thought of coming out to the park occupies a great deal of my time during the year. Itineraries are planned and then deconstructed only to emerge in new forms. Travel arrangements are thought out and made. Menus are created and supplies purchased. Re-supply boxes are prepared and mailed out. My pack, clothing and gear are made ready to hit the trail. Conditioning occurs so that I can enjoy and complete the hike. Then, once the trip is over, it will be a year or more before I see some of these grand sights again. This particular trip was great but leaving the island behind is always hard to swallow.

In looking back at this initial solo hike on Isle Royale some impressions remained clearer than others. Among my lasting memories of this journey were:

> 1. Hearing wolves howl from the Greenstone Ridge early in the morning. It is a privilege and an honor to have heard these sounds. The call of the wolves set my mind to thinking about the pack and all its activities.

2. Hearing the sound of loons and their varied & eerie calls. Every time I hear a loon call I stop whatever I am doing and feel a tingling sensation. Loons are a true vestige of the great Northwoods.

3. Spending time watching moose feeding in Washington Creek. This season there were far fewer moose on the island than in past years. To see some of the diminished herd at close range was memorable.

4. Meeting a fox on the trail and spending time sizing each other up. Foxes are fascinating creatures whose intelligence shows. I always enjoy seeing them, let alone making eye contact and communicating through body language at close range.

5. Hiking through the hottest days I have ever encountered on Isle Royale. I knew it was hot while I was walking but it was not until I reached Rock Harbor that I fully realized just how high the temperatures had been. According to the rangers it had been over ninety degrees every day that I had hiked on the ridges. In fact, at Houghton they had recorded all time high temperatures that skyrocketed up to ninety-nine degrees. No wonder I was drenched so early every day and left pumping fluid at a rate that surprised me. This had been tough hiking but I still felt strong at trip's end.

6. Seeing wildflowers that covered hillsides or peeked out from the undergrowth. The warm weather brought out Canada Dogwood, various orchids, and wood lilies in numbers I had not previously seen. It can be quite a lift to hike up a rocky hill and then be rewarded by a carpet of flowers growing freely.

7. Meeting people who share a passion for wilderness. Not everyone who comes to Isle

Royale is a dedicated environmentalist but the remoteness of the park does call for some level of commitment to even get here. As a result, visitors will meet some fine people—many of whom return to the island time & again.

8. Seeing the vistas from hilltops and ridgelines. It is hard work to get up to Isle Royale's high ground—but the return on that investment of energy is great.

9. Lying in camp at the end of each hiking day, feeling the combined relief of reaching the day's destination & the tingling fatigue of the daily effort. This was a demanding hike on familiar yet challenging terrain. Making this journey has helped me grow.

10. Watching sunsets and the stars at night. Simply observing the grandeur of this landscape set amidst one tiny piece of the cosmos can make being in the wilderness a spiritual experience.

The end of every journey is also the beginning of something else. Even though my long-term plans included returning to the park shortly to continue work on this text, leaving it was still difficult. But, all things end, inclusive of this part of the journal & the events chronicled therein. If I had learned anything from these solo hikes it might well have been that if you enter the woods, you will leave them changed. The nature of that change depends upon factors both internal and external to yourself. What we bring to a journey interacts with the travel itself. In the end, if we have made a reasonable effort, we will gain from the experiences and uncover positive changes in ourselves. Isle Royale is a fitting canvas to paint such changes now and in the future.

Part II: Hiking the West End With Family

"Nature is a personality so vast and universal that we have never seen one of her features."

- Thoreau -

Day 1 (Tuesday—August 8): Every trip has its own flavor & pace. Some are compacted into limited time due to various constraints. Others are leisurely and flow along in an easy way. This particular journey was set up in such a way that a strong pace had to be maintained to complete it, but flexibility was built into it as well.

On this occasion Kyle, my oldest son, and his companion, Sarah, accompanied me. Our trip was designed to cover those major trails that I did not hike in June's solo hike. More specifically, our itinerary included a night at Washington Creek, a boat ride on the *Voyageur II* to McCargoe, a hike down the Minong Ridge back to Windigo, re-supply via the *Voyageur II*, and then the completion of the Feldtmann loop.

This time out I made arrangements to fly the three of us into the island via the seaplane. On two previous occasions I had used the seaplane to reach the island. This would be a novel experience for Kyle and Sarah. Kyle had already been to the park on five prior instances. Sarah was a first time traveler to this remote place.

We drove up to Houghton from Illinois on Monday afternoon. Upon arriving in Houghton late Monday night we encountered unexpected difficulty in securing a hotel room. For some unknown reason every hotel and motel in the area was full. Eventually we were able to find a room in Calumet, about eleven miles north of Houghton. As we approached the motel we saw numerous lightening flashes out over Lake Superior. Later, at the motel, I went outside and watched the natural fireworks display. Lightning cut across the sky in a nearly continuous light show. Looking at that storm I wondered what the weather would be like out on Isle Royale.

The next morning the three of us arose and headed out for a meal in Calumet. After eating we drove out to the Houghton County Airport where we were scheduled to catch the seaplane for a 2:00 departure. Once we reached the terminal we read a posting that informed us that the morning thunderstorms had delayed all flights. We settled in and awaited the return of the seaplane's pilot for more information. At about 3:00 our pilot arrived and we boarded for our flight.

The seaplane owner operator is a young man named Jon who is a member of the Minnesota Air Guard. Jon is a veteran military pilot who specializes in flying F-16's. Jon served in Desert Shield as well as the many years during which American pilots enforced the "No Fly Zones" over Iraq. This was Jon's second year flying visitors to and from Isle Royale. Jon's business seemed to be solid and we felt more than comfortable in his experienced hands.

The flight out to the park took about thirty minutes and gave us a unique perspective on Lake Superior and Isle Royale itself. As we neared the island a thousand foot ore boat passed beneath us. Longer than three football fields, the huge vessel looked like a toy more suitable for a bathtub than a deep-water lake. Closer in to the island landmarks began to appear. I could make out Feldtmann Lake, the Greenstone Ridge, Siskiwit Bay, and the Minong. Memories of past trips to those places flooded over me. This would be my tenth trip to Isle Royale and each of those visits has had a unique tone. However, one thing all those trips had in common was that they each reaffirmed my deep respect for wilderness.

As our plane approached Washington Harbor we saw a female moose grazing in the shallows. As we were coming in to land the cow moose ignored us and continued looking for choice bits to eat. The moose population on Isle Royale was markedly smaller than previous years. Seeing a moose in our first moments in the park struck me as a good omen for our trip.

After departing from the plane we went over to the visitor center to register. We then headed down to the campground where we were fortunate enough to secure the last available shelter. We set up our gear and settled in at one of the nicest campgrounds in the park.

Washington Creek campground is set up along that narrow stream. There are eight or so shelters, some individual campsites, and a separate group site that sits along the winding shores of the creek. The area has abundant wildlife in it. If you choose to camp at Washington Creek it is well worth your while, bugs permitting, to sit outside and just watch the creek for a while. Any number of birds might fly or swim by. Moose often graze in the creek at almost any time of day but particularly in mornings and evenings. Red squirrels frequently run through camp and chirr at visitors. Foxes patrol the area and are often seen loping through camp or on the nearby trails. River otters may swim past as they seek out food or mischief. Raptors like osprey or bald eagles hunt in the creek and can be seen perching in the treetops. The pecking of woodpeckers can be heard in camp. If you are quiet you may even glimpse the Pileated

Woodpecker, the largest of its breed in the Northwoods, hammering away at dead trees. All in all, Washington Creek and the harbor it adjoins are prime areas to rest & observe wildlife.

Since today was a transition day with a late arrival we had limited hiking options. Arriving at about 4:00 left us with insufficient time to hike the 9.5-mile, Huginnin Cove loop as we had originally contemplated. Instead we chose to settle in, walk out along the trail leading to Huginnin for a ways, and get our gear & ourselves in shape for the real start of our hike the following day.

The remainder of our first day on the island was spent taking short hikes near and through the campground. Even on these mini-hikes we saw evidence of the lushness of Isle Royale. Despite the year's dryness, the forest stood out in its green denseness. We saw a pileated woodpecker pecking away and hopping from branch to branch in a dying tree. Moose prints were sprinkled along the creek's shore. At dusk the sun set over Washington Harbor leaving behind a tracery of pink and purple in the sky.

That evening we played the first round of a rummy game that was to last all trip. At dark we stepped outside the shelter and gazed up at a night sky full of stars. Standing there, looking up into the heavens, it was easy to feel part of some vast, inscrutable world brimming with unknown life.

Hiking Tips:
#60: If You are Hiking with Less Experienced People, Plan Well – In many ways the success or failure of a backpacking trip is based upon advance planning. This fact is even clearer if any member or members of your group is inexperienced or a novice hiker. In order to

have a safe and enjoyable trip for all participants, you must use your experience to plan in as careful a manner as is possible. Do not assume that an inexperienced backpacker will know what to bring, do, or avoid. Help that person before they reach the wilderness. Offer advice and assist them in terms of meals, gear, pack weight, clothing, and other key items. Do not patronize them but assist in whatever reasonable way you can so they can overcome their inexperience and become a successful backpacker. Remember, no matter how many thousands of miles you may have hiked, you too were a greenhorn at some time in the past. Hopefully, more experienced hikers helped you out as now you will serve others.

#61: If Possible leave some Flexibility in Your Itinerary – It may not be possible but if you can allow yourself a day or two of flextime in your plan, do so. If you can build such flexibility into your itinerary you put yourself, and your group, in a better position to cope with unpredictable factors such as weather, injury, or equipment failure. Flextime also allows you to modify your plan and spend more time at places you need or wish to. For example, if you want to spend a day simply hanging out at Washington Creek and have flextime in your schedule—you can. If you can manage it, flex time may dial down the pressure that can accrue from a tightly scheduled itinerary on a trip and give you the breathing space necessary to enjoy your vacation to the fullest extent.

#62: Listen to the Woods – It is easy to get caught up in the planning, effort, and challenge of a trip. But, if you are always pushing yourself, you may not be in the right mindset to take full advantage of just being in the woods. Periodically, simply pause along the trail and just listen to what surrounds you. Whenever you are in a place like Isle Royale you will be surrounded by life. Song sparrows offer their plaintive call. Squirrels scold you as an intruder. The wind pushes its way through the trees. Loons call out on an unseen lake's surface. Life registers in many ways. Stop and listen to the woods and you will be rewarded.

#63: Always have Time for Humor – During almost any hiking trip moments will come that challenge your will. Bad weather days will occur and test your mettle. Trails may prove more challenging than reported or remembered. Bumps and scratches can happen. Bugs can run rampant. Having good humor in the face of adversity is both a survival skill and evidence of maturity. As the days and miles progress it is important to see the humorous circumstances that life presents us with. When you think back to trail companions and people you have met whose company you enjoyed, it is unlikely that many of those folks were ill tempered. If you can share goodhearted humor with others you spread light at a time of potential darkness. Look back on your own memorable hiking mishaps, foibles, and miscalculations. Perhaps even retrospectively you can find the humor contained within those circumstances. Remember, laughing at adversity changes it into something you no longer need fear or dread.

#64: Do Not take Yourself too Seriously – Imagine yourself just completing an eleven-day trip from Rock Harbor to Windigo via the Minong and then back along the Greenstone. In so doing you have overcome obstacles and accomplished your goals. You feel pride and a sense of purpose. You have met the challenges set before you and life is good. These are all healthy thoughts. However, if they begin to slide into the realm of self-importance you are entering into dangerous and self-deceptive territory. Nothing we do is worthy of blatant egotism. The hiker who gloats above hiking the length and back of Isle Royale will eventually meet an Appalachian Trail through hiker. In turn, the egotistical AT through hiker may well encounter some one who has hiked all of the AT and the Pacific Crest Trail. Each of these people has completed a noteworthy journey. But none of them should consider their travels as supreme. In humility the hiker finds balance and comradeships. In egotism a person may well find only isolation, contempt and narcissism.

Day 2 (Wednesday—August 10): Our second day on Isle Royale started out on a high note. I had trouble sleeping so I was awake early when thumping sounds started to be heard just outside our shelter. I crawled out of my sleeping bag and took a look out of the screened shelter door. There, to my right standing about thirty feet away, was a mature cow moose. The moose was grazing and took no notice of me. I quietly called to Kyle & Sarah and the three of us watched her as she had her breakfast.

Watching a moose feed is a treat. They are highly effective eaters as they must be to ingest the 30-40 pounds of vegetation they consume every day. This female set about her daily eating tasks by vacuuming low growth vegetation and stripping tree and shrub branches. At this close range I could hear the moose's chomping as she set about her dietary work with gusto. Kyle and Sarah returned to their sleeping bags but I continued to watch the moose until she headed down into the creek. Once the cow reached the creek she splashed along and fed on aquatic plants.

Today is a change of base day. After getting up we planned on packing out and heading down to Windigo. There we were scheduled to board the *Voyageur II* and shuttle over to McCargoe Cove just as I had done in June. After this three-hour cruise we would then immediately set out for Todd Harbor thus completing the first of the four days we planned on spending on the Minong Ridge

Trail. This first day stood a good chance of being an excellent break in hike for our feet, gear, and us.

At 11:00 we boarded the *Voyageur II* for our ride to McCargoe Cove. It was a beautiful day with a mixture of light clouds and blue sky. The cruise along Isle Royale's north shore was once again rewarding. The ruggedness of the coast was a hard and fast testament to the power & ability of Lake Superior to carve and shape its world.

As we steamed toward our first true hiking day of this trip we passed loons and cormorants gliding across the water. Other cormorants flew just above the water in their commonly observed flight paths. Although many people in this region denigrate the cormorant, it is a fascinating element of this Northwoods realm. These birds have great prowess as fishers. They also appear like miniature sea serpents when you see them swimming along the water's surface. Their low flights offer up the living image of a ship borne missile cutting its way through the air just above the water. There may well be down sides to these dark feathered birds but they are here and thriving.

As the trail from McCargoe to Todd Harbor is described in part one of this book, I will not go into great detail concerning it. However, what was interesting was having the ability to compare and contrast how this portion of trail was in August as compared to its June status.

In June when I hiked this stretch of trail I did so in the early morning. On that occasion my early start helped me to avoid much of the heat and humidity that dogged me throughout that trip. Today, our start time was about 3:00 in the afternoon. The day was hot and moist. Although the temperatures were not as searing as they were in June, walking along the ridgeline was taxing. Early on in the hike I was dripping wet. By the time we reached Todd Harbor I was soaked in perspiration.

Luckily the heat diminished significantly at the lakeshore. A cooling north breeze lessened the humidity and made the evening perfect.

In June the bug population was soaring. All through that June trip I dosed myself with bug spray and donned my mosquito netting. Conversely, today we saw very few biting insects. When we stopped and took a sit down break we hardly noticed them. In camp they were nowhere to be seen.

The weather in June was fairly dry with the exception of one enormous thunderstorm that soaked the island. That combination of some rain and the heat brought out a veritable plethora of wildflowers. Hiking out to Todd Harbor in June I remembered the fields of wildflowers that spread out along the ridges.

In August after a very hot and dry summer, most of the ridges were scorched. Grasses once green and lush were reduced to brown husks. The thimbleberries sported desiccated and yellowed leaves. Large portions of exposed high meadows were dried out and dead. Virtually no wildflowers could be seen in that dry land.

Hiking in August also brought out more people. The *Voyageur II* was packed. Campgrounds where, in June, I had seen virtually no one, were full or nearly so. On the trail the three of us saw quite a few people heading toward McCargoe. We did have the trail to ourselves most of the time but we saw more people today than I did in essentially my entire June trip. Early summer, spring, and fall trips are for those who seek solitude. Hikes in high summer will result in more human encounters.

In terms of how we stood up to the rigors of today's hike, I would say it was a good start. Kyle led all day and set a fast pace of 3+ miles per hour. Sarah walked with determination and grit. This was Sarah's first true backpacking experience and prior to arrival on the island she had modeled some apprehension. Yet by day's end she kept up without complaint. Sarah, and fortunately all of us, ended the first day with no blisters. For Sarah, her first hiking day on Isle Royale was a hard but successful one.

When we reached Todd Harbor we picked out a campsite and hoisted our two tents. Camp chores were quickly done leaving time to sit on the rocky beach while the rolling surf washed up. Todd Harbor is a lovely place and I have always enjoyed staying there. The combination of its rustic beauty and isolation make it a "must see" place in this park. On a clear evening you will get a wonderful sunset if you can actually stay up long enough to see it.

As the evening rolled around our good fortune continued. The weather was cool and clear. After cooking and eating supper the three of us went down to the shore to watch a golden sunset. As the sun sank down behind one of the islands that guard the entrance to Todd Harbor we saw a long streak of gold in the water. As the sun dipped lower the scattered clouds became purple, pink, and red. Such a sight was both inspiring and humbling.

As darkness gathered we went back to camp to play cards by candlelight. The shimmering candles cast a honey colored glow to the game. In that warming glow our good fellowship and camaraderie grew.

At bedtime we departed to our separate tents. I settled in to finish Norman MacLean's *A River Runs Through It.* This is a wonderful novella, included in a book that also contains two other short works written by this former professor at The University of Chicago. As I read I also listened to three loons who were calling and responding to one another out in the harbor. The loon's unearthly calls & variations gave me pause. I lay in my tent and wondered if there was another wilderness sound quite so unique? Perhaps only the call of wolves has moved me more than the loon's chorus. What a fitting way to end a fine day in a great park.

Hiking Tips:

#65: Close Your Eyes & Pause – Every once in a while simply close your eyes and observe the sounds that surround you. As you do this, resist the temptation to analyze what you hear. When a bird calls do not wrack your brain to identify it. Instead, silently think to yourself, "I am hearing a bird." Bask in the sound rather than dissecting it. If you are lying on the shore listen to the sound of the waves and let their eternal melody ring true. If you periodically pause and just close your eyes in camp or on the trail you will be surprised by what you hear & how refreshing it can be. Experiencing nature is different than competing with or cataloging it. Take a few moments and just listen.

#66: Share a Familiar Place with a First Time Visitor – Returning to a park such as Isle Royale time and time again can be very satisfying. However, if you have the opportunity to accompany someone who has never visited your old stomping grounds, take advantage of the chance. Sharing a familiar place with an enthusiastic novice serves you well in two fundamental ways. First, your experience and knowledge can help another person learn to appreciate the wonder of a specific park. Second, the enthusiasm of a first time visitor can be contagious and rekindle your own level of interest. Therefore, bring a friend, relative, or other loved one with you the next time you hike the Minong, traverse the Greenstone, or walk any number of Isle Royale's beautiful trails.

#67: Only Use Bug Spray when You Need To – If bugs are thick by all means the use of repellant sprays is a must. But before you begin covering yourself with Deet, check out the need for it. It is wise to have adequate bug spray readily available. Yet, can you not wait until the need arises before spraying it on yourself and others? In late summer and early fall bugs are on the wane. In dry years insect populations may plummet and make them scarce even in their favorite seasons. Therefore, be a little cautious about using insecticides if you do not really need them. Remember, Deet is a poison, and we do not really know its long-term effects.

#68: Break In Easy – There is a common tendency to really push and hit the ground running at the start of a hiking trip. Time is a limited resource and many people want to cover as much ground as possible. As a result, itineraries can become overly ambitious. Mileage that seemed reasonable on paper suddenly becomes overwhelming in the real world. If you want to avoid painful disappointment, break in your trip with easier days at the outset. On your first couple days on the island you should resist the temptation to pour on the miles. At the start of a hike your pack weight is at its maximum, your feet are not toughened, joints are not accustomed to the terrain, and adrenaline can push you beyond where you should be. Use the first few trail days to warm up to the demands that backpacking in the backcountry can exert upon you. If you do so you will be both safer and more observant as you travel. A rushing hiker bent on "seeing everything" may well end up "seeing" very little and experience more pain to boot.

#69: Try to be Patient with Yourself & Others – If you backpack very much you will encounter annoyances. Beyond the natural challenges that may confront you there are also human relations issues. Noisy neighbors in camp, dawdling partners, litter on the trail, and any number of human interferences can mar your wilderness experience. However, people are part of the environment. You cannot let the discourtesies of others ruin your trip. If you encounter liter—pick it up & carry it out. If people you hike with become annoying—let them know, hike alone, or find a new trail partner. When people are unreasonably loud in camp—ask them to quiet down or ignore them. Every bad situation like these can certainly become aggravating. However, if we patiently reframe the circumstances they are more easily coped with. In coping we allow ourselves to enjoy the place we are visiting. In approaching problems in this way we also adopt a pattern of behavior that has far broader benefits than simply on the trail or in a wilderness camp. Problems can be reframed in almost any setting if we take the time to do so.

Day 3 (Thursday—August 11): Today we broke camp and hit the trail at about 9:00. My two trail companions tend to be late risers but we are trying to work toward earlier start times in order to avoid walking in the heat of the day. Our destination today is Little Todd Harbor, about seven miles west of Todd Harbor.

This portion of the Minong is one that I am fairly familiar with, as I have hiked it several times. Little Todd is a beautiful campground. The campsites are located very near the shoreline of Lake Superior. A curving & rocky beach stretches out along the harbor. If you enjoy looking at stones of all descriptions then Little Todd Harbor is the place for you.

Our hike began with about two miles of generally level trail. About 1.5 miles from Todd Harbor we came to the trail intersection with the spur pathway that leads over to Hatchet Lake. Hikers looping back toward Rock Harbor or veering over to the Greenstone Ridge Trail can make good use of this 2.5-mile trail. The trail is fairly moderate and takes a hiker around the eastern end of

Hatchet Lake to a campground and a steep access trail up to the Greenstone.

After about two miles the Minong began to become much more hilly. Every once in a while we would drop down to a creek, small stream, or wet area. These were generally bone-dry or much lower than usual. But, each descent was swiftly followed by a climb. In fact, this pattern of up and down walking was characteristic of this section of the Minong.

In terms of landscape features, much of this hike was through relatively open forest. The trail went through a mixture of deciduous and pine trees. Some of the more interesting forest sections were those that passed through birch woods. In those birch woods the light bark of the trees, the trembling leaves, and the gently suffused light made the forest seem serene.

One of the more pleasant features of this trail segment were the parts that allowed us to walk along hillcrests. On either side of us the ground dropped away to wooded gullies. Striding along those crests I felt almost like a low flying bird skimming the treetops.

While there were very few opportunities to see Lake Superior, occasional glimpses did appear through the trees. Unlike the bare rocky crests that we encountered yesterday in the first part of the Minong, this segment of the trail featured more enclosed wood walking. Yet, despite the more limited panoramic views, I have always preferred this second part of the Minong over the walk from McCargoe to Todd Harbor. The rolling deep woods nature of this part of the trail has always struck me as having more character than the more frequently traveled first phase of the Minong.

In terms of trail performance, Kyle led the way and maintained his rapid pace established yesterday. Sarah continued to demonstrate a strong spirit while holding her own. I followed so that I could lag a bit and watch for wildlife. Starting at 9:00 I did not think we had much chance of seeing moose, but fate is sometimes kind. I knew we would pass several beaver ponds and wet areas where moose frequently graze while attempting to remain cool. However, on this day none of the island's diminished moose population was in sight.

We did see a blue heron take off and circle a beaver pond. The heron's somewhat crow-like call echoed against the ridgeline that was on the other side of the valley containing the beaver pond. According to my mother's family who came from Germany, the sight of a stork or heron in flight betokened good luck. I took this sighting as a good omen and suspended any disbelief. I am not a very superstitious person but, in the wild, it is wise to accept help from any source.

During our trail break I helped Sarah tend to her feet. She had developed a couple tender areas so some preventative moleskin was applied. For a person who had never backpacked before she was doing a really good job of coping with a tough trail. It is hard to break into a hike and if you have little prior experience you may not realize that things get easier day-by-day.

After our break we headed into the final portion of today's hike. We began to get some good views of the Greenstone Ridge off to the south. We then came to a stretch of alders that grew up along a small creek. Nearby was an old beaver dam that bespoke past engineering efforts made by these intrepid builders. When we came to a creek crossing made up of downed logs I realized that we were fairly close to the spur trail leading down to Little Todd Harbor. One more hill climb and we came to that intersection.

At the trail marker we found a moose antler. It appeared to be a younger bull's antler but its weight reminded us of just how powerful these animals are. Bull moose dedicate an amazing amount of energy to growing, supporting, and using their antlers. These giant growths have essentially one purpose—the attraction of mates during the fall rut. Antlers can easily weigh forty pounds. They remain covered in blackened velvet skin until fall. Then the velvet is rubbed off in a bloody autumn ritual conducted by bull moose who have hormones surging through their systems.

The energy used to grow antlers and fight for mating rights is a prime reason why bull moose, on average, live about two years less than cows. The procreation imperative drives bulls to don their majestic racks and use them to win the right to pass on their genetic heritage. In some ways we might equate the bull moose's antlers with the prominently displayed muscles of an aggressive male human or the expensive car & stunning wardrobe of a rich and eligible bachelor. In both instances the male pays a one dimensional price by either working out to the exclusion of less narcissistic actions or focusing so much attention on material possessions that life can become shallow. Like the bull moose, an overly fixated human male lessens his life expectations and narrows his scope until it becomes tunnel vision.

Returning to Isle Royale, we hiked in to Little Todd Harbor and were greeted by a wonderful camp. We set up our two tents very near the shore and faced them into the wind so that last night's condensation could dry. In rapid order our tents were dry and we were established in camp.

In fairly short order we noticed that there were plenty of biting flies out and about. These bugs were nasty biters who sometimes drew blood when they chewed on us. We headed down to the shore and found that there were far fewer of these miscreants near the water. On the beach I soaked my feet and started looking at the rocks that surrounded me. Once you begin looking at individual rocks it can be easy to become pleasantly distracted. Each pebble or stone had unique features. Some were speckled like bird's eggs. Others had natural mergers of light and dark elements as if they were a real life reminder of the Taoist Yin & Yang symbol. Some stones were smooth to the touch and called out to be caressed. Others were more rough and jagged, featuring craters where mineral materials had sloughed off over the millennia.

Sitting at Little Todd and looking at a mere handful of the countless stones on the beach quieted my mind. I could imagine my wife, Jane, who loves rocks, spending days sifting through these stones & pebbles. Holding one pebble in my hand I realized that all elements of life are astounding. In no way could I truly fathom the forces of nature that crafted even one of these stones. In a very real way, holding one stone I was in touch with our planet's geological history. Long after I am dust, that stone will still be somewhere in or near Lake Superior. People sometimes speak of human creations as "timeless." At the same time as such words are spoken very little thought is given to the world around us and the things that have existed since the birth of the planet.

During the afternoon Kyle and Sarah spent time wading and swimming in the harbor. The water was fairly warm by Superior standards. It was nice to see my comrades having fun but my older bones quaked at the thought of immersing them in that ice queen of a lake. The future belongs to youth. My own future will probably never include a swim in the icy waters of Lake Superior. Oh well, to each his or her own pleasures.

Today was a successful day on several counts. We completed a tough portion of the Minong in good time & with good order. The weather was pleasant and cooperative. Our pace on the trail was sound & people recovered well. The woods were lovely and it was nice to see them again. Very few mosquitoes were seen, heard, or felt. Our campsite was scenic and dry. We arrived in camp by mid-day thus avoiding the heat and allowing for ample time to decompress and rest up for the tough challenges of the next two days on the Minong.

Our evening was spent playing cards and building a fire. Little Todd Harbor is among the minority of campgrounds that has a fire ring for each individual site. We gathered downed wood and got a reasonable fire going. As it was so dry out we were careful not to overdo our campfire ambitions. Seeing the flames of a campfire dance while smelling the wood smoke can be a real camper's delight. If you have a chance to build a fire at an official fire ring on Isle Royale and have the energy to do so, by all means follow through on your desire. Campfires can help create fascinating conversations, dreams, and memories.

Hiking Tips:
#70: When Hiking Downhill, Watch your Feet – If you are hiking downhill it is important to carefully place each step. On dry and pebbly terrain there is a very real chance of slippage. Many people ignore this terrain feature, and fall. Instead, by being careful about foot placement, you can more readily negotiate descending trails. Instead of simply walking downhill with your typical stride, try to place at least one foot sideways as a solid base of support. In this way your lead foot will be at right angle to your trail foot. The "L" position allows you more stability and leverage on an uncertain slope. In some instances both feet will need to be turned sideways with your body leaning backwards to provide a stable center of gravity. A downhill fall can be very dangerous. Be cautious with every step, make good use of your hiking sticks, take your time, and watch your foot placement

#71: Watch your Spacing on Ascents & Descents – If you are hiking in a group be sure to allow sufficient space between people on ascents and descents so that one person's mishap does not become a trigger for a chain reaction meltdown. If you are too close to the person in front of you who is climbing and he or she comes tumbling down they probably will bowl you over. Conversely, if you are twenty or so feet behind them, instead of at their heels, you could act as a "spotter" and help them while maintaining your own safety. As on the highway—do not tailgate.

#72: Place your Least Experienced People in the Middle of the Pack – In sports it is the norm to groom a young athlete for success. A top quarterback drafted into the National Football League out of college usually serves an apprenticeship on the bench as a reserve. In backpacking, it is poor practice to have a novice hiker either lead or trail a group larger than two. In the lead, an inexperienced hiker may have difficulty establishing a consistent pace or recognizing trail hazards. As the trailing hiker, a new comer may actually get separated from the group or lost. Additionally, a novice trailing the group can make mistakes that go unnoticed. Less seasoned hikers have things fall off their packs or out of their pockets. If they are the last hiker no one will notice and the dropped materials are lost. Like musk oxen, put the less experienced members of the herd in the middle of the group.

#73: Take Breaks after Tough Climbs – On any sort of long hike you will take breaks to rest, recuperate, and drink. There is a tendency, particularly among less experienced hikers, to take a break part way up an ascent. Try to avoid this tendency if you can. Of course, if you are climbing or descending much of the day you may not have much choice. However, if you have an option, take your break at the summit. In this way you maximize your enjoyment and sense of privilege. Also, your break will come after a significant expenditure of energy and effort.

After your break you will be walking on easier ground. The oxygen and caloric deficits that are tiring your body can more readily be overcome on more moderate terrain. Gradually, over time, these deficits will lessen as you achieve trail conditioning. Psychologically, it is also much easier to hoist your pack and head out onto a more gentle terrain. Think about it, which would you prefer, starting up after a break on flat land or in the middle of a five hundred foot elevation gain?

#74: In Dry Weather do not Take Water for Granted – If you have hiked trails before it is easy to become negligent in terms of your preparation. Just because there were plenty of filtering spots along the way in June does not mean that they will still be there in August. In hot weather be sure to start hydrating the evening before a hike. Then, just before setting out, drink a good amount of liquid. Carry two full liters of water and do not count on all typically occurring water sources as being viable filtering points. Drink as needed on the trail but on hot days shorten the time between water breaks. If you come upon a viable water source top off your bottles and carry the weight. In camp begin to replace lost fluids as soon as possible. If you experience cramps or other signs of dehydration—drink and rest. Hot weather can truly challenge a hiker. Do not make the natural challenges of terrain and temperature lethal by ignoring your hydration needs. Also, be aware that water sources shift with the seasons and cannot be taken for granted.

#75: Take Time to Readjust your Pack along the Way – It is very common to make adjustments along the way to both how your pack is fitting and the way your gear is stowed away. What seemed like the perfect fit or arrangement back home may not be optimal once you are in the field. For example, on several occasions on Isle Royale I have felt the need to readjust my pack load. Loosening or tightening some straps or moving items around made me feel better and more effective as a walker. If your pack does not feel right—stop, readjust, and reap the rewards of your diligence.

Day 4 (Friday—August 12): Last night featured a steady to heavy rain that carried on into the morning. Isle Royale needed the rain and we were happy to be in our watertight tents. A couple of times when the rain let up a bit I could hear moose snorting and grazing nearby. I tried to see them from the front of my tent with my headlamp, but was unable to do so. I did spy several bats as they swooped through camp in pursuit of insects. Later that night I was awakened by an animal sniffing just outside the bottom left vent of the tent. By the time I was able to get my headlamp on it was long gone. I believe it was a fox looking for food.

We waited for the rain to abate and broke camp at about 9:45 and headed for our next destination—North Lake Desor. The rain and dew had left ample moisture on the undergrowth. By the time we had hiked the slightly more than half-mile spur trail back to the Minong our clothes and boots were soaked. As we left Little Todd Harbor behind I thought about how beautiful it was there. Let me once again stress what a striking campground Little Todd is. If you have a chance to stop there, by all means make a point of doing so.

The hike to North Desor was one of the more unique ones in the park. If you look at the map of Isle Royale you might wonder why the campgrounds established at Little Todd and North Desor are so close together. Our hiking distance today was going to be slightly less than six miles. That is a very moderate distance and could cause an inexperienced hiker to scoff at the day's work. If you actually walk this portion of the Minong, this mileage issue will clarify itself for you.

Virtually the entire trail leading up to North Desor is a rock climb. Most of this hike involves climbing up to rocky crests, walking along their uneven ground, and then climbing back down the rocks to valleys. The distance between Little Todd Harbor and North Desor is short because this is a very taxing walk. This fact is particularly true if the rock is wet as it was on this day. In that moist circumstance every single step must be carefully thought out prior to being made. The combination of slippery rocks and wet boots can make it feel like you are ice-skating as much as hiking. In such circumstances you have to expect slips and prepare for falls. On this day I slipped and caught myself once while Kyle followed suit with two near falls. Only Sarah, our novice backpacker, made it through all day without a spill.

This part of the Minong is practically mystical in its beauty. The hiker encounters an almost Alpine landscape, with frequent views of Lake Superior and Canada beyond. Our hike began with threatening skies and a strong wind. On the clear ridges the cold wind from Superior complemented the harsh yet stunning landscape to make for a striking walk. Along the rocky crests we could look down into small valleys and out across to the Greenstone Ridge. All in all, there may be no better stretch of trail in the park than this one.

As we walked along toward North Desor we encountered only one other group of hikers. Even during the island's peak season it is only a minority of backpackers who choose to walk the entire Minong. In a way this is reasonable as the terrain on the Minong is more challenging than the other long trails in the park. But if you are adventurous and fit, you will not find a better hike in the park than the Minong.

Once again, Kyle led the way today. He continued to set a strong and rapid pace. His fitness was good and his weight was lower than it had been in years. That combination made him a strong hiker. Sarah held up well and continued to demonstrate a spunky and big-hearted attitude. I did well but the continued humidity caused me to drink far more fluid than I usually do. Hydration is vital so I drank both along the trail and in camp.

One of the hardest demands this trail section makes on hikers is the almost constant rolling nature of the terrain. The climbs up to the ridges, and in particular the longest one about halfway to Desor, are tough. The Minong was originally laid out as a backcountry fire trail. Therefore, it lacks the number of switchbacks that other trails in the park provide. Many of the climbs on the Minong are head on collisions rather than the serpentine walks evident on the Greenstone or Feldtmann Ridge Trails. Further, up on the ridges, there always seem to be large step-ups and step-downs that stretch hamstrings and sap energy. By day's end we were all soaked and ready for camp.

As you near the half-mile side trail to North Desor camp you will first begin to see the valley where the lake rests. A long rocky descent with another sharply textured &steep hill up ahead on your right will lead you into a marshy valley. A bit more rocky ridge will take you to a final descent at the foot of which rests the trail to North Desor. The daunting hill that you last see just prior to this final descent will be part of tomorrow's hike wherein you will ascend its backside and skirt that hill's depressing steepness.

The half-mile trail to camp was a gently descending one that led us through a lovely birch wood. North Desor camp has only three sites but each of them can accommodate two or three tents if need be. The campsites are located on a hill overlooking Lake Desor. Although clambering down to filter water requires some balance, coming to Desor and sitting by its shore is rewarding.

Desor is a beautiful wilderness lake. Loon calls echo over its surface. The Minong and Greenstone Ridges embrace the lake. Trees line its shore giving it a true Northwoods feel. Often the wind will kick up white caps as it pushes its way along the water. Birch trees whistle in the breeze. Clouds scuttle past giving the weary hiker an opportunity to simply sit, stare, and meld with the woods. Lake Desor offers much to those hikers who pay the price of effort required to reach it.

After reaching camp we set about completing chores. Kyle and I set up the tents in the sun to dry them after last night's showers. Sarah went downhill to filter water from the lake. I laid out our wet clothes and boots to dry. Shortly thereafter we settled in to cook a multi-course meal that featured sweet & sour pork, vegetarian lasagna, hot chocolate, broccoli-cheese soup, and almonds. All three of us were very hungry and aware of the need to carb up for tomorrow's long day.

A side note on food—Sarah is a vegetarian and finding single serving dehydrated entrées for her was a bit of a problem. However, there are several excellent dehydrated vegetarian meals available. These entrees generally come in two person helpings so be careful in your planning. These meals are very tasty and I will go so far as to say that they surpass most of their meaty counterparts in terms of flavor while having similar caloric & nutritional value. Even if you are not a vegetarian a mixture of these meals with your other menu items certainly can provide a hiker with variety without sacrificing nutritional content.

After dinner we settled into a routine of talking, reading, writing, napping, and card playing. It has always been a privilege to hike with my son, Kyle. The addition of his girlfriend, Sarah, has added rather than subtracted from the mix. Such opportunities to share time, effort, comradeship, and good company with others are rare. I was glad to be in this wonderful park with people who appreciate it and one another.

Tomorrow's walk will be out to Windigo, a distance of approximately thirteen miles. Along the way we will hike up and on rocky ridges, through deep woods, in boggy areas, and down a fair number of hills. This will be a tough but multifaceted hike. It will also be a gift to have the opportunity to walk these miles again.

Hiking Tips:

#76: Bring a Deck of Cards – If you stroll around a campground at Isle Royale you will come across people playing cards. The games being played may vary, but hours will be dedicated to shuffling cards, dealing them out, and playing them. After a long day card playing is a good way to quietly pass the time. On a long trip a continuous game of rummy, spades, or pinochle can enhance the journey's fun. Cards weigh virtually nothing and stand up well to the rigors of the trail. The next time you go out to Isle Royale, or any park, stick a deck of cards in your pack and let the games begin.

#77: Bring a Headlamp – Candles certainly add a romantic and/or ethereal touch to camp but you cannot burn them safely in your backpacking tent. In the dark you will struggle to find things if you do not have a light source. In fact, it is amazing just how dark it can get in a wilderness area like Isle Royale. Therefore purchase, pack, and bring a headlamp. If you are a good planner you will also bring spare batteries & know how to replace them. At night, when you need to find an item, a headlamp will be appreciated and will allow you free use of your hands.

#78: Beware of Leeches – It may be tempting after a hard day on the trail to take a dip in Hatchet Lake, Chickenbone, or McCargoe Cove. Backpacking on Isle Royale can be a sweaty, foot pounding, and gritty experience. What a good idea to rinse off or soak your tired body. If you do so in any number of the park's inland lakes or bays be aware that leeches are not uncommon. I have seen leeches swimming in plenty of locations and have had them attach themselves to me a couple of times while soaking tired feet. Leeches are somewhat revolting but generally harmless creatures. A leech will be attracted to your soaking foot or dangling ankle. If you find a leech on you do not panic. Usually grasping them will be enough to trigger their release. Leeches are not ticks who, if pulled out, may leave mouthparts behind in the wound that can cause infection. Many times if you pull on a leech it will release. Your wound may bleed for a while due to the anti-coagulants that leeches use to assure a swift blood flow in the wound & to their waiting mouth. Staunch the bleeding with pressure, sanitize the small wound, apply antiseptic cream or ointment to the wound area, and bandage the wound. Leeches are somewhat disgusting but they are part of the natural order. Thus, if you enter into their home turf, they may pay you a visit.

#79: After a Bad day on the Trail, At Least Change your Socks – This suggestion is a bit of a paraphrase taken from Norman Maclean's wonderful book *A River Runs Through It.* Each of us probably will have days on the trail where everything appears to go wrong. If you are having one of those very bad, terrible, horrible no good days change something at day's end. Your socks are one option. Another could be your attitude. The lesson to be learned is that bad times can be the precursor to good ones or more bad ones. To a great extent, the determination of good or bad future karma rests with us. Change something around and set the stage for better days on the trail and in life in the future.

#80: Respect Boiling Water – Most backcountry cooking essentially involves boiling water and adding it to something. When I am backpacking, and especially when other folks are with me, I find myself boiling a lot of water. It is easy to ignore dangers that are common and close to home. Handling boiling water is just such a common danger. Be very careful when you have a camp pot full of boiling water. It is all too easy to overturn it or grasp the pot with insufficient insulation. I remember on one occasion accidentally spilling some hot water on my foot while cooking. Luckily I had a camp shoe and socks on. I was able to whip them off leaving just minor sunburn on my foot. However, things could have been much worse. Do you really want to be in the backcountry, miles from help, with your foot blistered from second-degree burns? Always be careful when boiling water. First, select a level surface to do your cooking. Have at hand a towel, glove, or some sort of potholder that will protect your hand when you pour. Do not engage in horseplay when cooking. Keep young children away from the boiling pot at all times. If you should spill boiling water on you immediately remove all soaked garments. In this way you can at least minimize the time that your skin is exposed to high temperature. If burning has occurred, cool the area with purified water or soak as needed. Apply antiseptic cream and bandage the burned area. Do not break any blisters that appear. Be familiar with first aid basics for burns. When able, walk out and seek medical help or send a sound member of your party to do so. On Isle Royale that could be a long walk and a time consuming process. If you have to leave the injured person in camp be sure another person stays with them to support them. If the injured party must be left alone make sure they have water, shelter, food, and some kind of medical kit inclusive of analgesics. The easiest thing to do is use common sense around boiling water in the first place. One simple mistake with it can not only ruin your trip but also create a very dangerous situation.

Day 5 (Saturday—August 12): Sitting in camp at the end of a long day I wrote these words outside shelter #13 while by the shores of Washington Creek. Across the creek and to my left a cow moose grazed along the far shore. The 6:00 PM sun shone down and helped make her look like a decorative, silhouette moose you might see displayed in someone's front yard. But she was so real.

The water dripped from her great head as the cow moose lifted it to chew her choice morsels nudged from the creek bed. Powerful thighs moved slowly, deceiving the observer by hiding their potentially fierce strength. Ears went up and rotated independently as the moose periodically checked her surroundings. Then, once she felt comforted, the cow returned to her eating. The splash of hooves as she moved up the stream signaled her departure from my view. But, I will always cherish that encounter and the place it occurred.

Windigo, and its adjoining Washington Creek Campground, were our ultimate destination today. Hours before that moose encounter occurred, we got up and hit the trail at about 7:45 in the morning. The thirteen-mile day and the tough terrain motivated all three of us to get up earlier than had been the norm for this trip. We anticipated about six hours on the trail inclusive of breaks.

The portion of the Minong that runs from North Desor to Windigo is a virtual potpourri of the entire trail. The first two miles after the intersection with the North Desor feeder trail features the scenic but gritty rock climbing so typical of the segment running from Little

Todd Harbor to North Desor. Much of the walk from North Desor to Windigo runs through rolling woodland much like the hike from Todd to Little Todd. The many big views that are periodically offered up along this final leg of the Minong are similar to those encountered on the stretch between McCargoe Cove and Todd Harbor. Yet, while this final part of the Minong has distinct elements of the three preceding segments, it also has several unique features.

Between North Desor and Windigo hikers will climb at least eleven significant hills. In addition, there is a generalized roll to the ground that saps you as the day plays out. In wet years, the marshy parts of the trail that are a prominent element in the middle of the hike can be both messy and extremely buggy. There are three places along the trail where the hiker has to clamber over beaver dams that make up portions of the pathway. These crossings vary in terms of difficulty dependent upon water levels, rain, and trail conditions. On dry days they can be awkward but doable. On very wet days they are treacherous. Descents and climbs are generally more pronounced than other parts not only of the Minong but also any other prolonged stretch of trail in the park. These climbs occur throughout the hike but are most evident in the first couple miles out of Desor and in the middle portion of the hike. If you are hiking from east to west, which is the most common and recommended route, you should feel good after you descend from a barren area about four miles from Windigo. After that barren land you will climb one more big hill beyond and then head on to a final few relatively easy miles of your day.

In regards to our day on the trail, it could justly be described as productively challenging. Our early start was a wise move as it allowed us to avoid climbing most of the hills we encountered in the heat of the day. Also, as it proved to be a drier and less humid day than yesterday, our hike along the ridgeline crests was much less difficult. Climbing the rocky hills was tough but we were rewarded with some memorable views of the Canadian shore and Lake Superior's blue expanse.

After hiking through the Alpine first leg of the day's hike we took a drink break while sitting on a rocky hill. We then saddled up and headed on into the rolling forest of the trail. Once hikers finish with the rock climbing about 2.5 miles from North Desor they are afforded a bit of a reprieve from the arduous elevation changes. While these next few miles do included some woodland hills, much of this land is relatively level and easy to walk. This trail segment is also quite striking as the gently rolling path takes hikers through birch and other deciduous glades that are very lovely.

When we walked through this woodsy stretch we periodically broke out into meadowland. Here, as in many places along the Minong, we spied ripe raspberries. These red and juicy berries were delicious & I found myself periodically snagging a few along the way. These delicious woodland treats were certainly appreciated as I found myself walking along with the taste of ripe raspberries in my mouth and the red juice trailing down my face.

About 4.5 miles into our hike we began to follow a pattern that continued for at least half of the day. We would walk along level to rolling ground, descend to a wet area or beaver pond, cross over the obstacles, and then moderately to quite sharply ascend the next hill. Generally the hills we were called upon to climb would immediately confront us after the wet area to be traversed. In this way we walked through boggy areas or clambered over the beaver dams only to find a steep climb as the reward for our efforts.

As previously noted, the dryness of the summer left the boggy areas generally dry and harmless. The beaver dams, which sometimes have water spilling over them, were tricky but far easier to handle than on any previous hike I have made through this land. While this drought year had been terrible for farmers and forests, it made our hike much simpler. In the great scheme of things our minor needs were not really very important when compared to the destructive power of a drought. But, as we walked along in dry boots when we could easily have been soaked, we counted our blessings.

We took our second break up on the desolate area know as "The Barrens." This hilltop features many destroyed trees that render a harsh look to the landscape. A combination of fire and storms seem to have knocked down or killed the large trees that once dotted this rocky crest. Sitting there in my soaked hiking clothes I felt both fatigued and supremely comfortable. My tired state was the natural result of the trials and tribulations of the hike. My comfort was more complex.

At the most basic level it is a good feeling to know that you have broken the back of a difficult hike. Once the most arduous parts of a hike are behind you there is a combined sense of accomplishment and relief. There is also comfort in simply spending time in a wilderness area that has required effort on your part to reach. Lying on my back with the wind sweeping over me and the blue sky above me, I felt at peace. Wilderness can offer so much to people who venture forth to touch, see, smell, and taste it. What a tragedy it would be if humanity lost such places. There is nothing but tragedy wrapped up in exchanging such lasting necessity for temporary gain.

Following a wonderful and rejuvenating rest we set out on the final leg of the day's walk. Only one more hill had to be climbed, followed by a fairly easy and scenic woods walk. At one point we heard a whistle sound and I conjectured that it was the ferryboat, *Wenonah*, arriving at Windigo. I then estimated that we were about two miles

108

form our destination. A few minutes later we came upon a trail marker that informed us that Huginnin Cove lay 3.3 miles to our right, while Windigo was 1.8 miles to the left. We turned left and rambled on into the campground where, later in the day, I was destined to meet the moose mentioned at the start of this day's entry.

Once in camp we were again fortunate enough to be able to lay claim to a shelter. Clothes were set out to dry and housekeeping chores ensued. About fifteen minutes after our arrival I saw an osprey alight on the very top of a pine tree directly across the creek from our shelter. I spent some time eyeballing this marvelous raptor as it watched the creek with great intensity in search of food. Ospreys are sometimes referred to as "fishing hawks" as they use their magnificent eyesight to swoop down and capture fish. This particular osprey did plummet down on a fish right in front of me. Sadly, for the osprey, it caught but dropped a fish as it ascended for the far shore of the creek. The osprey then chose to perch back on top of the same pine tree prior to swooping down in order to retrieve the wounded fish that was splashing on the creek's surface. Much to the raptor's dismay, a shrewd seagull flew into sight, skimming the creek's surface, and snatched the injured fish out of the water. The seagull quickly continued on in its flight path and headed out toward Washington Harbor to my left. All the surprised osprey could do was scold the seagull with a chirping call and look chagrined.

One more word concerning osprey is that they are virtuosos of aerial acrobatics. Ospreys ride the wind and periodically hover high above the water. When they do this sort of hovering their strength and agility is obvious. Ospreys dive in a soundless way that is spectacular to see. Watching an osprey is a rare treat and one to be savored & prolonged if possible.

After observing the osprey for a while longer I heard a splash to my right. A female moose had emerged from the forest across the creek. The cow moose was feeding along the shoreline accompanied by snorts, splashes, and water dripping off her elongated face. She was the first of nine moose seen either from our shelter or around the camp that day. These seemingly cumbersome but in actuality strong, swift, and agile animals are always amazing to see. Windigo was the place to see moose this year, as it had been so many other times I had come to the park.

The remainder of our evening was spent eating sandwiches at the camp store, playing cards, reading, and writing. Washington Creek is a great place to get lost in observing or contemplating wildlife and a simpler life. Not only is the moose population larger in this area than on much of the island, but there are also manifold birds & other creatures about. Virtually every time I have sat in front of a shelter at Washington Creek and just waited a bit, I have seen something pleasing. For example, on this particular evening, I chose to write at the picnic table in front of the shelter. I brought my headlamp with me as it was starting to get gloomy. First, several bats flitted by me at very close range. Then a wood mouse scampered by me along the wood planking that made up part of the external structure of the shelter. Using my headlamp I was able to watch this little fellow as it searched beneath the table for crumbs left by prior campers. The little mouse was very serious about its business as it went about earning its keep for the day. Every wildlife encounter does not have to be dramatic. This mouse, like myself, was but one humble creature. Yet, meeting it was a pleasant surprise.

Tomorrow's itinerary includes canoeing for Kyle & Sarah and a hike along the Huginnin Cove loop for me. We had decided to lay over at Windigo for an extra day.

We thought a day off their feet would be good for Kyle and, in particular, Sarah. Kyle's strength on the trail had been pronounced but he was a little footsore. Sarah had been a real trooper but her left foot had become fairly blistered. A rest day can be heartily appreciated and should set the stage for our successful negotiation of the Feldtmann loop.

Hiking Tips:

#81: Travel with Kindred Spirits – When you go backpacking to a place like Isle Royale you enter into a world marked by a much more primitive level of existence than is typical of everyday life. In the wilderness you will share joys and travails with the people or group that you hike with. Since you will be spending a concentrated amount of time with the person or people you hike with, be sure they are folks you really want to spend such focused time with in a wilderness area. For example, if you are looking for peace and camaraderie in an environment that you love, do not come to the park with someone who does not believe in the "Leave No Trace" philosophy & who never stops talking. Like in a marriage, choose your partner well and be sure of your compatibility.

#82: Double-check Camp before Leaving – Have you ever broken camp only to realize a half-mile or more down the trail that you left your hat behind in camp or stuffed your glasses in with your tent? Embarrassing though it is to admit—I have. Always check and double-check camp before you leave it. Taking that little extra bit of time to check over the ground or your shelter can be well worth your while.

#83: Respect All Life – On Isle Royale there resides a multiplicity of life forms. Each of these entities has a purpose and is valuable. In some cases, like mosquitoes and black flies, it may be difficult to appreciate them, but they are part of the island's web of life. By showing respect for all life we demonstrate one of the deepest spiritual values that exists. The tree that you rip branches from rather than taking the time to gather downed wood will suffer from your actions. The rotting birch log that is full of slugs should not be callously thrown into a campfire. Toads and crawling insects along the trail were not made to be stomped on. Let other living things be so that they can lead their lives as they were destined to without your interference. On Isle Royale, or for that matter in your own backyard, life abounds. In each and every place we have a choice to make. Do we value and respect life, or not?

#84: Bring Spare Bootlaces – Imagine that you are hiking the remote Minong Ridge Trail along Isle Royale's rugged north shore. Your bootlace is shredded when you slip and tumble on some rocks. What will you do? Well, if you packed spare laces you can stop, dust yourself off, make a simple change, and hike on. If not, you are going to have to creatively improvise. Your improvisational skills will affect your feet. Remember, perhaps no other part of a hiker's body is as important as his or her feet. Bearing that reality in mind, put a spare set of bootlaces in your pack and make life simpler.

#85: Carry the Lessons of the Trail Home – Many hikers go off on their trips and leave loved ones behind. They think of their hiking world as separate from the real world. The lessons they glean from their hiking adventures and on the trail do not generalize to family, home, and work. In reality, what is learned in a wilderness world like Isle Royale should transfer to our life in general. If hiking along the Greenstone makes you feel humble, cannot that emotion be applied to what you owe family and friends? If the sacrifice and sharing needed to safely hike from Rock

Harbor to Windigo and back inspire you to value teamwork, can you not reflect on how hard colleagues at work apply themselves to tasks with you? When you remember how moving a sunset at Todd Harbor was, can you apply that same emotion to your children's needs? The lessons of the trail have a place in the wild, within our hearts, and at home.

Day 6 (Sunday—August 14): I got up early this morning to head out for a day hike along the loop trail leading out to Huginnin Cove. This was to be a bout a 9.5-10-mile walk with its approximate midpoint being Huginnin Cove. The cove is similar to Todd Harbor but on a smaller scale. The campsites at Huginnin Cove are scattered along its edges facing out toward Superior from Isle Royale's north shore. Beyond the confines of the small cove, stretch out the blue waters of the great lake with Canada on the horizon. The mouth of the cove is perhaps fifty yards wide with the shoreline being quite rocky.

I left Kyle and Sarah asleep in the shelter. As I headed out I placed a note by the shelter door to remind them to pick up the re-supply box from the *Voyageur II* when it docked at 1:00 if I should not be back by then. In all probability I planned on being back in camp before the ship's arrival but, as the old adage says, "An ounce of prevention is worth a pound of cure."

As I hoisted my pack outside the shelter I heard splashes out in Washington Creek. A cow moose was tromping along down the creek right in front of the shelter. I watched her splash and feed for a while and then set off for my hike.

There is a good feeling that I associate with hitting the trail in the early morning. Yes, the morning dews and damps can be drenching, but the feel of the fresh sunshine and moist air is bracing. Birds are out and their calls can fill the sky. Trees and undergrowth glisten with the dew. Few people tend to out and about as island hikers tend to get later starts. The morning temperature is generally cool. Many animals are still out feeding as they try to beat the summer heat. All things considered, I believe that early morning is the best time to hike and a prime time to enjoy the woodlands.

As I was leaving the Windigo area on the trail I heard a moose feeding up ahead in the pines. I slowed down and carefully surveyed the area up ahead of me. In short order I spotted her. The moose and I stared at each other for a while and then her ears went back & her fur seemed to bristle. I sensed she was at least apprehensive so I backed away, spoke in a low & quiet tone, and stepped behind a tree. The moose then settled down and returned to her feeding. I was then able to observe her for a while prior to continuing my hike.

A word about moose watching and safety. Seeing a moose on Isle Royale is one of the biggest thrills in many people's visits to the park. But there is no joy in aggravating an animal that weighs more than a half-ton. If a moose seems uncomfortable with your presence, back away or step behind a tree. Moose know what human beings are, as we are annual seasonal visitors much like loons and Merganser ducks. They will probably be reassured to hear your low toned voice and realize that you are not a dangerous predator. However, if you surprise a moose, if it is the fall rut, or if you come across a cow with her calf or calves you must be extremely careful. What may seem like a wonderful vacation moment to you can be viewed by the moose as a direct threat or territorial incursion. Use common sense and enjoy the presence of these great creatures in safety.

My hike out to Huginnin Cove was great. The day was clear and cool. I enjoyed setting my own pace and walking alone. Once again, there were luscious ripe raspberries along the path. Periodically I snatched a handful and made a breakfast of them.

The hike out to Huginnin can be made in a clockwise or counterclockwise direction. Most people suggest counterclockwise as that route makes the first half of your hike the longest with your return being somewhat easier. I have always walked the loop in a clockwise direction so that the scenic stretch of boulder-strewn trail just east of the campground starts off the second half of the hike with a bang. This is purely a personal choice, as either direction will get you back to the same place—Windigo.

The trail leading out to Huginnin Cove is fairly rolling. Some of the hills in the first leg of the hike will challenge a hiker's conditioning. There are also steep and switchbacked descents that can jolt knees. However, this is by no means a killer trail.

As I walked through the generally wooded terrain I felt rested and centered. I had thoroughly enjoyed the companionship of my hiking partners but walking alone is a treat as well.

On my way out to Huginnin I saw a number of red squirrels up in the pines and along the trail. Many of them were chewing through the stems of dozens of pinecones. After the cones dropped to the forest floor the reddish whirligigs raced down the tall pines in pursuit of their food. Once on the ground the squirrels snatched up pinecones and ran off to store them.

For humans August is high summer. In the world of the red squirrels on Isle Royale, August is the harbinger of cold autumn and bitter winter beyond. Squirrels all over the island were storing up, fattening themselves, and bracing for the onslaught of winter. Others, like one we saw at North Desor camp, were grabbing mouthfuls of dried leaves and duff to pad & insulate their homes. Hard as it may be for humans in August to think about winter's far off frigidity, for squirrels, there is no choice but to plan.

As I neared Huginnin Cove I caught a glimpse of Lake Superior off in the distance. At that point on the trail I was about 1.5 miles away from the cove. A few hills, some wet areas, an old dry beaver pond, and some interesting stone cliffs met me just before I arrived at the campground.

The prior year in June when I hiked out to Huginnin I found not one single person either in camp or on the trail. Today, every campsite was taken and a fishing boat was moored on the dark boulders that make up the west side of the cove. This was peak season in the park and Huginnin Cove represents one of the more approachable locations on the western end of the island. Yet, despite the "crowd" the cove remained beautiful, just as I remembered it to be.

As I looked out over the cove the fishing boat began to pull out. Two little boys who were camping with their parents on the east side of the cove gleefully explored the rocks along the shore. Each pebble or stone they found interesting brought forth exclamations from them as they rushed over to their mom and dad to share their treasures. Nearby a young couple dried their tent on the rocky shore as they quietly sat shoulder to shoulder and stared out at the lake. Sitting silently here while all this human behavior surrounded me felt good. People who are observant can become part of the environment when they come to a place like Isle Royale. Watching, listening, and sharing with people you encounter can be part of the adventure as much as observing moose or scaling heights.

After spending about an hour at Huginnin Cove I packed up my gear and headed up the eastern portion of the loop. The first mile just east of the camp is one of the more interesting ones in the entire park. The trail is surrounded, and in some places consumed, by large boulders. On one side the hiker can peer down at the steep and rocky shoreline. On the other side a wall of craggy rock extends up toward the sky. Pine trees grow directly out from the stones and tangle their roots among the rocks. This can be a really stunning walk through what appears to be a different geological age.

Once I finished this rocky patch I headed up a hill and back into the woods. The eastern half of the Huginnin loop continued the patterns of rolling terrain that is so typical of this park. Raspberries were again evident and continued to be good eating. After a bit, I came to a beaver pond that looked promising as a moose habitat. Unfortunately, none were present on this day but I certainly believe they can be seen here. The trail then continued up and down until I came to the remains of an old miner's cabin. About a half-mile or so further I came to the old Wendigo Mine that was in operation from 1890-92.

At that historic site I was able to touch the rails used to move mine carts about. The skeletal remains of a second miner's cabin were at that spot as well. I walked through the doorway of the roofless relic and stood within the structure for a while. One can only stand in awe of the amount of work necessary to make a mining operation work in such a rugged and remote location. As I stood in the log cabin ruins I paused and wondered what had happened in this building. How many games of cards might have been played here? What type of gear & equipment was stored here? Did folks eat in this room, seated at a rough-hewn table? There were no answers, only questions.

From the Wendigo Mine site I hiked on past a large meadow area that had the look of an old beaver pond. Then, further woods walking brought me to the intersection of the Minong Trail and a relatively easy hike back to Windigo. On the clear downhill sections of this part of the trail I picked up my hiking sticks and jogged. It felt good to step out and speed down these final easier bits of trail. While I certainly do not recommend throwing caution to the wind or racing your way through the wilderness, sometimes it is refreshing to kick up your heels a little bit.

Back at the shelter I grabbed a few empty ration bags as well as my pocketknife and headed down to the dock to meet the *Voyageur II*. Our re-supply box of food had to be retrieved and I planned on immediately transferring it to our food bags. Then the box could be broken down and discarded on the boat. We would be ready for the next three day's hiking without any excess food weight or unnecessary garbage.

Sitting on the dock I looked around me and was once again struck by the beauty of Washington Harbor. I watched as a bald eagle hung in the sky before plunging down into the water. The eagle then pushed off with its strong wings and headed into the woods with a fish gripped in its talons. Nearby cormorants swam in search of food or comradeship. The blue water and sky complemented the forest greenery. Simply put, I was in a lovely and vibrant place. In a place such as Washington Harbor, on a remote set of islands such as Isle Royale, it can be easy to lose and find yourself. Sitting on the dock I remembered past personal triumphs and defeats. Each of these emotionally charged moments in my life surged up from memory. It was as if the healing balm of this special place allowed me to process what I needed to in a way that made sense. Most people have memories that haunt or help them. Perhaps, through letting oneself experience the natural order in wilderness settings such as Isle Royale, a person can achieve greater balance in daily life. It can only be hoped that this is true.

I was able to meet the *Voyageur II* and secure our food box. The crew was gracious enough to allow me to throw away my cardboard box on board the ship once I had transferred the supplies into our grub bags. I have nothing but praise for the *Voyageur II* folks, as well as the men and women who staff the *Ranger, Wenonah*, and *Isle Royale Queen* as well. They work tirelessly and provide fine service.

Back in camp after retrieving our supplies and chatting with some other hikers as well as Ranger Valerie I settled in to cook lunch. Food was then rearranged among the three food bags. Creek watching then followed these activities. Within a few minutes I heard the cheeping call of an osprey overhead. The osprey flew into sight and aggressively dived at the top of a pine tree across the creek. To my surprise a mature bald eagle sat atop the tree. Four times the osprey dove down at the eagle. Both birds brandished their wings and attempted to look as large as they possibly could. Finally, the eagle gave way and retreated out toward Washington Harbor. The osprey proudly took the spot & sat there with raptor dignity. The osprey's territory had been defended—a rival rebuffed. These fishing grounds were the osprey's and it would give ground to no other aerial predator.

The day closed with several rounds of cards, shaving, washing hair down by the public restrooms near the visitor center, and some more time sitting by the harbor. Kyle and Sarah returned after a day canoeing out to Beaver Island about a mile or two down the harbor. They had fought against a strong wind to pull their way out to the wooded island. We had a good time in camp talking about their watery adventure and my land bound travels. While we communed in camp moose grazed down the creek, woodpeckers beat a steady rat-a-tat in the woods, loons called out in the harbor, and the setting sun glittered on the creek water transforming it into a river of gold.

There are many transcendental moments in life—the birth of children, marriage's gentle touches, and deaths. But simple moments in uncommon places can touch us as well.

Hiking Tips:

#86: Leave No Trace – Stressing this park service tenet again is important not accidental. Human beings who visit a national park create an impact simply by being there. Even the most conscientious hiker leaves footprints behind. In order to lessen our impact upon the land it is essential for every backcountry visitor to embrace the "Leave No Trace" schema. Pack out all you garbage as well as other people's litter that you come across. Follow appropriate backwoods etiquette in terms of the disposal of cooking, fish, and human waste. Do not take souvenirs from the land. Bring home only memories and photographs. Leave behind only the slightest trace possible of your presence in the park.

#87: Honor Campground Rules – Imagine hiking to a remote camp like Little Todd Harbor only to be surrounded by loud people who have no respect for your privacy. You have little recourse in such an unfair circumstance. Honor camp rules in regards to being quiet and courteous. Reduce talking to a lower tone than you normally use in a crowded shopping mall back home. It is a wilderness setting where noise is minimal. You need not shout to be heard. Refrain from slamming shelter or privy doors. All you have to do is hold on to the handle until it closes. Hearing the sound of a shelter door slamming in the wilderness can set my teeth on edge and will win you no friends in camp. Quiet down after dark. Isle Royale offers some hard miles to travel. Respect other people's need for rest and sleep. Rather than disturbing them by talking into the wee hours, go to sleep and hit the trail early the next morning. You will avoid the heat and might even see some wildlife on the trail if you are quiet. Remember as Lao Tzu wrote in the Taoist classic *The Tao de Ching,* Much talk means much exhaustion; Better for it is to keep your thoughts."

#88: Make Camp & then Relax – If you can overcome the fatigue that you feel from the trail it is recommended that you set up camp as soon as is practicable. Filter water, pitch your tent, and make camp once you have the energy to do so. Then you can get into dry camp clothes and relax, knowing that you have the basics of life in order. Rest well and bask in the forest's sounds without anxiety of work left undone.

#89: Do not See Life Through a Lens – While it is important to bring a small camera along to catch a trip's "magic moments" you should not dedicate too much thought to it. Unless you are an avid and adept photographer many, if not most, of your photos will not really do justice to the mountain, woodland stream, or ridgeline you are trying to capture. Have a camera with you but do not obsess about what your next picture should or could be. In the wilderness there is no way to schedule a "photo-op". Live in the present moment and enjoy what you see. If you lose sight of the beauty of the wilderness because your mind has become an extension of your camera's lens, what have you accomplished by hiking the trails?

#90: Give Way to Uphill Hikers – If you meet other hikers on a graded trail and you are descending, give way to the climbers. Backpacking in hard country is tough enough without losing all forward momentum while going uphill. Yes, going downhill can be joint crunching, but the rule of thumb is to make way for those folks gaining elevation.

Day 7 (Monday—August 15): Once again, I got up well before Kyle and Sarah. The morning was brisk and clear. A thin mist trailed along above Washington Creek. As I prepared a breakfast of oatmeal I heard sloshing in the creek. Yet another cow moose had emerged to the left of the shelter. I ate breakfast along with the moose. Both of us felt the early morning sunshine begin to warm the day.

While I sat there with my oatmeal gray jays flew through the camp looking for human leftovers and more natural prey. One of the bold jays landed on the picnic table where I was sitting and surveyed the camp and me. Gray jays are intelligent and feisty. They make up a part of the "camp police" that patrol the campgrounds and seem to be able to find the least crumb left by humans.

We got started with our hike fairly late at about 9:30. Our goal for the day was Feldtmann Lake nine miles away. Feldtmann Lake is a popular west end destination for backpackers. It makes up a thirty-mile loop and is a common trip that many visitors make. Feldtmann is also a typical component of longer hikes that include the Greenstone and/or Minong. Many people also make Feldtmann a multi-day stopover point.

The hike out to Feldtmann Lake from Windigo is not a difficult one. For the first mile the path hugs Washington Harbor and is very level. Then, just as you come to a point where you are parallel with the end of Beaver Island and its dock, the trail turns sharply inland and begins an uphill slog. This climb up to the ridgeline is much more progressive than those on the Minong. However, by the time you reach the top of the hill at a small rocky knob, you will be breathing harder. Once you pass those rocks you will look down into a valley through which Grace Creek flows. Beyond the creek a small unnamed pond is in view. To your right and beyond the ridgeline you will be able to see Superior and a portion of its shoreline.

At the ridgeline you will pass an unmarked spur trail that leads off to the left into the grass. I suggest you follow it for about 100 feet or so to a rocky overlook. From this vantage point you will have a much more satisfying view of the valley than can be garnered from the main trail. This is a good spot to take a drink and look down at the creek, valley, meadow, pond, and successive ridges beyond.

After pausing at the Grace Creek overlook we pushed on. The trail slightly ascended before taking us along the ridgeline. Then we descended into woodlands and then some open country. Here, parts of the trail were covered in lake stones. At a distant time in geologic history this land was covered by that era's version of Lake Superior. Centuries and centuries ago this land was either lake-bottom or shoreline. Then, after the last glacial age, the water receded until the present shore configuration was set. The stones were left behind and now they make a rather incongruous pathway. However, it was interesting to realize that the stones we strode upon were once part of an ancient shoreline or seabed.

From this point we dropped down to the bridge crossing over Grace Creek. The creek is fairly modest but represents a fine filtering point if you need water. Also, the area around the creek often plays host to moose, and bulls in particular. In past years I have been fortunate enough to see several large bulls just beyond the creek crossing. It is strongly suggested that you walk quietly and with observant eyes & ears during the miles between Grace Creek and Feldtmann Lake.

As it was, shortly after this point I had to briefly separate form my trail companions. My indulgence regarding the consumption of ripe raspberries over the past few days had finally caught up with me. Nature called and I had to stop to answer. Perhaps ten minutes later I caught up with Kyle and Sarah who had gone on ahead. I found them stopped along the trail. As I neared them they quietly informed me that a bull moose was standing in the middle of the trail just ahead. I looked just beyond them and there he was.

Seeing any moose is a thrill but sighting a bull is much more infrequent. This fellow looked to be perhaps six or seven years old. He had a sizeable rack that was still covered in dark velvet. His dewlap was still somewhat short but his general appearance was quite healthy. His dark coat was full & sleek. No areas of rubbed off fur could be detected. He did not have large grape-like tick infestations. The bull appeared to be strong and well fed. Everything about this fellow said, "I am boss here and no one can push me around." We watched the bull for a while as he grazed near, on, and beyond the trail. Photos were taken and, when it appeared safe, we walked on past the big fellow.

From this point all the way to Feldtmann Lake the trail was essentially flat. Calling this trail a "route" would be very fair as our greatest challenge during the final five miles of the hike were the manifold roots that covered much of the trail. Much of our attention was drawn to these tree roots that snaked their way all over the trail. Looking down became habitual as the roots frequently waited for any unaware moment to sneak up and trip us.

The last half of the walk from Windigo to Feldtmann traverses pleasant but somewhat redundant terrain. By and large hikers have forestland to cross with dense undergrowth hugging the path. You will know you are getting near the lake's campground when the path starts to have smaller lake stones strewn across it again while the woodland opens up a bit. When we finally reached the marker for camp we took a left and headed along the spur trail that led directly to the sites. Only one site was taken and we were fortunate enough to claim the double site at the far end of camp. From there we were able to see not only the lake but also the Greenstone Ridge in the distance. Our tents were less than twenty feet from Feldtmann nestled among some pines.

After setting up camp we soaked our feet in the lake. Sarah's ankle was bothering her as she had twisted it during a fall about a mile or so outside of camp. All three of us enjoyed sitting on the pebbly beach with our feet and ankles in the cool water. We had hiked through from Windigo without a break and made the trip in less than three hours. I felt strong and smiled at the thought of possibly seeing loons on the lake.

Once camp was set we cooked a big lunch, ate, and talked. Everyone's humor was fairly good. The setting was beautiful and as we looked out at the lake a pair of loons emerged. We also noted that the sky was clouding up. We agreed that if rain was destined to come it was much better to be comfortably in camp than still out on the trail.

Looking out across Feldtmann Lake at the distant ridge it was easy to feel at home. The absence of any other campers on the beach accentuated the peace and isolation of the moment. I recalled my first visit tot his spot years ago. At that time I had never been to Isle Royale. Feldtmann Lake was the first place I ever camped in the park. Little did I then know how many times this wilderness park would call me back to it.

As afternoon progressed toward evening the sky began to clear. We could hear Lake Superior's surf pounding over at Rainbow Cove, slightly less than a mile from camp. Rainbow Cove is a lovely spot that can easily be reached and makes a nice side trip from Feldtmann Lake. There, set against Lake Superior's power, is a curving beach that offers vistas, a majestic place to rest, beachcombing opportunities, and an amphitheater to watch magnificent sunsets. A trip out to the cove from Feldtmann is strongly suggested and can be made in ten to fifteen minutes with ease.

Sitting next to my tent, among the moss-covered pines, I looked up into the sky as clouds passed overhead. Gnarled roots from the larger trees nearby crawled near me like pythons only to burrow into the earth beneath my tent. The peace of the site seeped into me like a naturalistic IV. I thought about writers like Sigurd Olson, John Muir, and Thoreau. These artists had seen wild places as avenues to which they dedicated much of their passion. I also thought about my family back home and how much they meant to me.

We can become prisoners of our possessions. Backpacking reduces life to very simple terms. You walk—you see—you eat—you drink. Life on the trail revolves around a barebones essence. In the wilderness there is no forgiveness for poor planning or falsehood. You cannot fake your way over a ridgeline as you might a presentation at work. Life is objective and clear. But there is also beauty, suffering, hope, reflection, and grandeur. I hope to gain from this trip and the experiences it reveals to me. I also long to share those experiences and that growth with others as a way to repay the island for all it has done for me.

By about 7:00 PM I had played some cards and spent time looking all along the beach near camp. At that time two loons came close to shore. The loon couple alternately dove, surfaced, cruised, and preened. In a relatively short amount of time this mated pair will separate. Loons form a close pair bond that is lifelong. However, males and female winter in different far off seas. There, separated from their mates, they molt their striking black, white, and red plumage. At sea the loons don a rather drab gray and white coloration while they lead their solo life. Time passes and, in the spring, the loons return to their chosen nesting sites hopefully to rendezvous with their mate and raise a chick or two. How sad to think of a solitary loon returning to its wedding spot only to find no mate there to join them. I wonder what loons think and feel in those sad circumstances? Do they have questions in their mind about the missing spouse? What does that loss do to their heart and mind?

Aside from the loons I also watched a blue heron patiently hunting along a reedy part of the shoreline. Herons are supremely capable stalkers. They stretch out their long neck, prepare their spearfish bill, and carefully survey their domain. Blue herons can stand patiently and still for long periods of time. Then, when prey is sighted and zeroed in on, their head darts forward to snag an unsuspecting fish or frog. The heron's stealth is pronounced, as is their hunting prowess.

As time passed I felt the urge to walk the mile or so out to Rainbow Cove. Kyle and Sarah were content to remain in camp and commune, so I set out alone. The walk to the cove was level and easy. In short order I had reached the broad and arching pebble beach. The sky was partly cloudy but unthreatening. The repetitive surf pounded in as if to remind me of the lake's latent power. I lay down on the rocks in solitude and gazed out into the ocean-like setting.

Tomorrow our plan involved hiking out ten miles to Siskiwit Bay. Our journey moved toward its conclusion just as each one always does. But, there remain miles to cover. As I went to bed I prayed that they would be good and safe ones for each of us. Night came, and the stars shone above our tents. A mist formed on the lake. The night sounds cascaded down on us and acted like a woodland lullaby. There are far worse places to be than in your tent at the conclusion of a good day in the woods.

Hiking Tips:

#91: Stretch – If you are an athlete, or exercise regularly, you know that stretching before a demanding activity is advised. Muscles and tendons perform their jobs better if they are prepared for the demands created by exercise through gentle stretching. Therefore, you would be wise to stretch before you hit the trail. Key areas to stretch are hamstrings, calves, back muscles, shoulders, and feet/toes. If you choose to refrain from stretching prior to a day's hike you increase the chance of fatigue, strain, the possibility of a pulled muscle, or spasms. Stretching should be gentle, prolonged, and not involve bouncing. Simply find a tree or wall to push against. Then successively engage in a short stretching regimen. If you do not stretch you are taking an unnecessary risk. You are also making it harder for your body to break into the start of a hike. If you wish, stretching after a trail break or at the conclusion of a hike can also help tired muscles channel off lactic acid and thereby lessen aches and pains. The bottom line is, your body is part of your gear. Treat it with respect and it will perform better. Neglect it, and problems will find you.

#92: Turn Your Liner Socks Inside out Before wearing them – This may seem like an odd tip, but I have found it to be helpful. Over the course of a day a backpacker takes thousands of steps. Any irregularity in a hiker's socks or shoes can cause hot spots or blistering to develop. Even the best liner socks have narrow thread lines on the inside. By simply reversing them, you lessen friction between the liner sock and your foot. Such a reversal has no effect upon the liner's wicking performance. Why take even the slightest risk of getting a blister if you do not have to?

#93: Appropriately Dispose of Human Waste – If you have to go to the bathroom in the backcountry there are some fairly basic principles that apply. If urinating, step off the trail a fair distance and complete your task. Do not urinate within one hundred feet of any water source. If you have to use tissue, pack it out or dispose of it at the next available privy. If you are creating solid waste, go off trail at least fifty to one hundred feet. Then dig a small hole about six inches deep. Deposit waste in said hole. Refill the hole with earth and arrange the ground cover so as to disguise the hole. Pack out paper or dispose at the next privy you come to. If you follow these common procedures your impact upon the park will be neutral to negligible. What you do not want to create is a disgusting and unsightly mess for other hikers to encounter. Also, and in particular during Isle Royale's dry season, do not attempt to burn tissue. Fires are started by this kind of behavior and the results can be catastrophic.

#94: Hike on Durable Surfaces – Much of Isle Royale's lovely terrain is fragile. Think about the delicate mosses, lichens, ferns, and wildflowers that live along the island's ridgelines. Thousands of thoughtlessly placed & tromping boots can, and will, exert a tremendous effect upon these life forms. Stay on the trails. Try to avoid stepping on living plants or delicate rock structures. Try to resist the temptation to skirt every mud hole that you encounter. Such walking will worsen erosion and make the mud holes worse. Of course, weather and trail realities will necessitate some course corrections. Only the most diehard hiker will slog through every slough that dots the trail landscape. Use good judgment but try to stay the course to the greatest extent possible. Every hiking stride you take that stays on the designated trail helps to protect the park. Every stride off the trail tramples to dust a little piece of this great park.

Day 8 (Tuesday—August 16): Thunderstorms last night and in the early hours of the morning dampened things a bit. However, our tents were sound and we weathered through well. What the rain did accomplish though was to wash out any thoughts of an early start to our hike out to Siskiwit Bay.

I was the first member of our party to arise. As I walked through the trees to take a morning look at the lake I glanced over to my right. There, emerging onto the beach simultaneously with me was a bull moose. The bull was about seventy feet to my right and paid no attention to me. He briefly glanced my way and then sauntered into the water. The bull then waded his way out to the reeds. Once there he flopped his head around in the water and began to graze.

Seeing a bull moose first thing in the morning made me feel good about our day. The sky was clearing and the day was looking up. I woke up Kyle and Sarah and we set about the task of breaking camp. We hit the trail at about 9:50 and entered into a world of wet foliage and slippery roots. The walk along the edge of Feldtmann Lake was lush. The trees and undergrowth were covered in moisture. The sunlight reflected off the plant life and gave the woods a distinctly glittering look.

Beyond the far end of the lake the trail first progressively, and then steeply, climbed its way up to the ridgeline. After making that hard climb we stopped at the overlook and gazed back at Feldtmann Lake. From that fine vantage point we could also see Lake Superior, Rainbow Cove, our old campsite, and the ridgelines that snaked their way across the island. The wind off the lake cooled us after a tough hike. We stood there silently and took in the elaborate view that nature and our efforts had provided to us.

From that high point the trail generally followed the open ridge for one to two miles. Occasionally we dipped back into the forest but typically we were able to stay out on the open ridge. Unlike the Minong, walking along the Feldtmann Ridge was generally level and fairly easy.

About three miles into our hike the trail turned into a woods walk. At that point we hiked through dense deciduous growth. At one point we skirted a beaver pond that looked to be inactive. Shortly thereafter we passed some huge boulders and exposed rock near a small waterfall that was very impressive.

Our midway break point was the Feldtmann Ridge fire tower. Shortly after emerging from the forest we caught a glimpse of the tower up ahead of us. After that first glimpse we walked another half-mile or so before we came to the grassy hill where the tower sits.

After hiking through from Windigo to Feldtmann Lake the previous day without any break, we pledged not to repeat that strategy on this day. We honored that pledge and took a relaxing rest at the foot of the tower. Socks and boots were removed and partially dried in the sun. Snacks were taken out of the upper parts of our packs and consumed. Water and Gatorade were refreshingly drunk. We also walked up the tower for a panoramic view of where we had been and where we were headed. All in all, it was a fine rest at a good spot.

The second half of our day's hike had two distinct flavors. For the first two miles we descended off the ridge through a combination forest that featured some wonderful stands of birch trees. As always, the birch trees made the trail seem serene. Those trees help create an atmosphere of ease and made for a fine walk.

About three miles short of Siskiwit the trail began to follow an old logging road. Here the trail narrowed and fluctuated between an open meadow and a woods walk. For much of the way the early afternoon sun beat down on us. The path was closely lined by undergrowth making it difficult to impossible to use our trekking poles. From past years I remembered this part of the trail as one of the more mundane and redundant sections of the park. My memory served me well and we hurried on toward Siskiwit Bay.

The campground at Siskiwit stands in sharp contrast to the somewhat boring stretch of trail leading up to it from the west. There are two shelters and we were fortunate enough to get one. The camp is set up to face a broad bay that opens out into Superior. On rough days, if the wind is blowing from the west, Siskiwit Bay can kick up its heels and be very impressive. On any day, its clear and cold water is a nice place to filter fluid and soak tired feet.

We settled into our shelter, made camp, and cooked lunch. Afterwards we napped to the sounds of the wind and the surf. Generally I am not a napper but today it felt good to sack out for a while after walking for miles under the hot sun. When we awoke Kyle and Sarah went down to the shore to filter water. Kyle returned shortly thereafter and informed me that they were having some problems with the filter. Kyle asked our only neighbors to borrow their filter while I disassembled and then back flushed ours. Clogging in the cartridge was evident. This had probably been caused by our having to filter from several beaver ponds along the Minong where mud and silt was heavy. At any rate, a little tinkering allowed us to use our filter.

Our evening was dedicated to carrying on our ongoing rummy game. Sarah is an adept cardsharp as well as being very competitive. She has surged into the lead in our trip-long contest and appears to be a sure winner. Playing cards down by the dock, watching the sun dip below the tree line, and hearing a loon call from out in the bay all made for a fine way to close out another good trail day.

As it darkened I walked the shore, looking at the rocks. This bay can have many moods. Tonight's was a peaceful one. I headed up to the shelter where the three of us ate our last powdered soup mixes. We lit our remaining five candles and talked into the night. Each of us felt good about our hike, the things we had seen along the way, and this fine park.

Hiking Tips:

#95: Know how your Water Filter Works – In the backcountry water is a precious commodity. A reliable water filter is a must. Sometimes filters malfunction. Bearing that glum reality in mind, it is essential that you know how to assemble and disassemble your water filter. Back flushing with some models can allow you to remediate the ill effects of silt buildup from prior filtering in murky waters. Beaver ponds and other gritty water sources can overwhelm your filter. If you know enough to revitalize your water filter, or at least get it to limp along until journey's end, you will have done well. If not, then you are in a very difficult place.

#96: Know Something about your Destination Before you Arrive – Did you realize that moose have only lived on Isle Royale for about a century? Were you aware that a massive forest fire in the 1930s blackened most of the western and central portions of the park? Can you name the fifteen mammals that live in the park? Do you know what part of the year is Isle Royale's peak time for berry picking? The mere accumulation of arcane facts for their own sake is an arid activity. But, knowing something about the flora, fauna, history, weather, geology, and topography of a place like Isle Royale can better prepare you for a visit in two main ways. First, knowing what you are getting into will help you to better plan and prepare for a trip to the park. For example, if you know that early June can be a very buggy, cold, and wet time, you will pack your gear accordingly. Second, having some understanding of the place you are visiting can deepen the actual experience of being there. Knowing that wolves use many of the trails you will walk along is a powerful thought. Understanding how protective moose mothers are of their calves is a lesson to learn before you arrive and unknowingly upset a cow moose weighing over a thousand pounds. Knowing some of the human history of past island residents broadens the impact of mine pits, historic buildings and the areas where people tried to carve out a livelihood that you will encounter along some of the trails. The more you know about a place the more you can learn when you get there.

#97: Understand Basic First Aid – One of your group members twists an ankle while walking along the rocky Minong Ridge. Your comrade is in pain and the ankle appears to be badly sprained. What do you do next? If you have no idea how to proceed in this hypothetical situation you are taking a grave risk every single time you enter into the backcountry. Most backpackers have no medical training. Yet, it is easy enough to take a basic first aid class, read a first aid manual, and develop at least some rudimentary grasp of first aid basics. It is advisable to carry a first aid pamphlet or small guidebook with you in your pack. It is also recommended that you carry a reasonable first aid kit with you whenever you backpack or day hike. As part of that kit it is recommended that you carry lightweight ankle and knee supports. The last thing you should want is to suffer an injury, or have one of your companions do so, with no one having any idea what to do about it. Oh, by the way, in case of sprains as in the opening gambit to this tip section, remember the acronym RICE. This pneumonic device stands for:

Rest
Ice
Compress
Elevate

#98: Follow your Itinerary as Closely as You Can – When you register and receive a backcountry permit you will inform the park staff of your itinerary. Of course, plans change and you may not follow your initial itinerary exactly as planned. But you should try to stay with your original game plan to the greatest extent possible. In an extreme situation, wherein you are incapacitated, it would serve you and your loved ones well to have the park staff know you are overdo and where you might be found. Also, in the unlikely but possible scenario that park staff are called upon to find you because of some sort of family emergency off the island, they will be unable to do so if, at the last moment, you decided to hike the Minong Ridge rather than the Greenstone. Make a plan, report it to the rangers when you register, and stick as closely to it as you can.

#99: Help Others if They Need It – If a fellow hiker's water filter fails would you refuse to help them filter water simply because it creates more work for you? On a day of heavy rain would you refuse to share your shelter with another hiker whose tent leaks? If a person in camp is suffering from blisters and has neglected to pack moleskin would you refuse to share some of yours? Hopefully your answers to these three hypothetical questions would be a resounding "NO". The backcountry is a hard enough place to function when everything goes well. When misfortune strikes, it can sometimes seem overwhelming. If you can lend a helping hand to other people, always do so. By extending yourself to help others you really help two parties. First, your help allows other people to safely complete their journey. Second, the good deeds you do help you as well. Remember, an honest gift helps both the recipient and the giver.

Day 9 (Wednesday—August 17): I awoke in the morning to the sound of clomping hooves. As I got out of my sleeping bag I saw a moose behind the bushes directly in front of our shelter. On closer inspection I saw that it was a mature bull with a large rack. I woke up my comrades and we watched the moose graze and then run off. What a good way to start off our final day on the island.

Last days on Isle Royale are always a mixed blessing. On this morning I was unsure as to when I might return to the park. In the back of my mind I had some thought of making a fall trip to add another dimension to this book. However, that trip was far from a certainty. I might not return to Isle Royale until next spring or summer. It was even possible, though hopefully unlikely, that I would never return to this park. I had enjoyed my time out on the island this season but all things must pass. In a retrospective way I began to think about the highlights of this particular trip. As this thought process continued I began to make a mental list of those high points:

1. Seeing a mature bull moose at close range near Grace Creek.
2. Watching a determined osprey at Washington Creek where it soared, perched, fished, and scared off a bald eagle.
3. Seeing the magnificent views of Lake Superior and Canada from the Minong.
4. Eating delicious raspberries along the trail.

5. Hiking from North Desor to Windigo in under six hours—what a tough hike but one that I felt refreshed from.
6. Climbing over the boulders and rocks east of Huginnin Cove on a piece of trail that is unique and a treasure.
7. Watching moose graze in Washington Creek and just sitting by the stream waiting for things to happen.
8. Looking out at Lake Desor on a windy day. This backwoods lake has always inspired me and with white caps kicking over its surface it was most impressive.
9. Looking at rocks on the shore of Little Todd Harbor.
10. Watching the sun set like a golden orb at Todd Harbor.
11. Sitting at Rainbow Cove while the surf pounded in on the rocky beach and Superior stretched out to the horizon.
12. Walking through birch woods and feeling close to the spirit of this place.
13. Looking across the stillness of Feldtmann Lake with the Greenstone Ridge in the distance.
14. Hearing loons and feeling a strange wonder at their calls.
15. Sharing this place again with my son, and for the first time with Sarah.
16. Hearing the rain patter against my tent while knowing that I was safe and dry.
17. Watching a seagull carefully pick berries at Siskiwit Bay. This gull reminded me of a shopper at a grocery store—checking fruit for ripeness—taking some while leaving others.
18. Watching a mother moose scold her recalcitrant calf for dawdling at Washington Creek.

19. Feeling the joy and work of hiking and the relief of dropping my pack at day's end.
20. Watching a tireless red squirrel gather pinecones, harvest leaves, and prepare for the rigors of winter.

Every trip has a flavor, and this one had been a delicious one. The absence of bugs had been an enormous plus. The rains we had encountered had been at night. Our days were generally clear or partly cloudy. The stifling heat I had experienced in June only dogged us on a couple of occasions. Wildlife had been much more obvious than in June. Campgrounds had been far less crowded than anticipated. All things considered, this had been a fine trip.

Today's hiking plan featured a walk up to Island Mine, then down the greenstone to Windigo, and finally a rendezvous with the seaplane for a 5:00 departure. The hardest part of the hike promised to be the tough climb up past Island Mine to the Greenstone. The Greenstone section of the hike would be a fairly easy way to finish off our trip as it gradually descends toward Windigo.

As we prepared to leave camp I saw three loons flying overhead. As they flew past I heard them periodically call out to one another. The unusual sight of the loons in flight stuck with me as we headed up the trail toward Island Mine.

The first portion of our hike was right along the bay. We chose to walk on the beach rather than fight through the tall grasses on the narrow trail. So we strode along in the sand with the waters of Lake Superior literally lapping at our feet. By simply turning my head to the right I could look out at the gray waters of Superior stretching out to the horizon. The wind blew in off the lake and cooled us as our bodies broke into the hike.

We continued our walk on the beach until we briefly turned inland to cross Caribou Creek. This creek was named in honor of another member of the deer family that once flourished on Isle Royale. The caribou have been supplanted by the moose who, in turn, are hunted by the wolves. Things change in life not just for human beings, but also for wildlife.

We then crossed the Big Siskiwit River via a substantial footbridge and continued to hike along the lakeshore for a while. Then our pathway turned inland toward the Greenstone Ridge. At the turn in the trail I paused for a few seconds and offered a silent thanks to Lake Superior for the good fortune we had been given along its shores. I also recalled the odd fact that the first time I hiked this part of the Feldtmann loop I had been disappointed by it. Subsequently, I have grown quite fond of the hike up to Island Mine.

If you choose to take this hike you will begin your move away from Superior towards Island Mine along a fairly level trail leading through forest. Then the trail begins to roll a bit with a steady but moderate uphill grade. About a mile or so into the walk the ground begins to slant upwards at a steeper angle. Your breath begins to speed up as the climbs become steeper and closer together. Finally, just before the homestretch to the Island Mine Campground, you encounter a long & steep hill. After half way up this hill you will cross some open rock before taking the last steep climb. This particular climb is one of the most demanding hills in the entire park. If you climb it you will feel a sense of accomplishment.

When we finally ground our way up to Island Mine we took a refreshing break at the campsite that Kyle and I stayed in during our first trip to the island. As we sat there in our dirt and sweat encrusted clothing we talked a bit about how difficult the life of a 19th century miner must have been on Isle Royale. Near the Island Mine Campground you can look at the old mine pits and tailings. To think about those miners lugging equipment and ore up and down the hills that tested us was difficult to imagine. Those same miners battled the insects, weather, and other elements that Isle Royale can throw at people. Every bit of the miner's gear and food had to be shipped across the temperamental waters of Lake Superior. Even though the mines generally failed in short order, that fact does not undercut the fact of the hard work of the miners who sturdily carved their place in the island's history.

When we concluded our break we got up and walked about a half mile further up the trail until we came to the intersection with the Greenstone. From that point to Windigo was 6.5 miles of sequentially descending trail. The entire walk was through a forested area. While this was a nice woods walk we found ourselves pushing the pace. Each of us wanted to get to Windigo with a little time to relax and recover prior to our seaplane flight back to the mainland. With that thought in mind we blew along, passing several hikers en route. We covered the seven miles from Island Mine camp to Windigo in an hour and forty-five minutes and still felt strong at the end.

At Windigo we slid into shelter #13 where we had stayed the two nights prior to heading out to Feldtmann Lake. We changed into our camp clothes and put our hiking gear out to dry. I really wanted some time to sit by the creek and watch for wildlife one last time on the trip. I also wanted some quiet time to think about the events of the past nine days.

As I sat at one of my favorite spots on Isle Royale I reflected on the hike and the companionship I had felt. I really feel proud of Kyle and enjoy hiking with him. Over the years he has steadily developed into a strong backpacker. Kyle is a trusted trail companion and a good comrade in the wild.

Hiking with Sarah, a novice who I really did not know very well, had originally concerned me. The Minong is a difficult trail for an experienced hiker let alone a rookie.

But Sarah handled the trip well. This development reinforced a fact about hiking, and life in general, for me. Given the right support, a motivated person with at least rudimentary skills can succeed at even the most difficult task. An inexperienced hiker should not attempt a tough trail like the Minong alone or with other green backpackers. By coming with people who knew the park fairly well and could reasonably equip her, Sarah was ahead of the game. But an effort like that still required inner strength and heart to carry her up and over the many hills we crossed. Sarah demonstrated this type of heart as she coped with every demand the trail threw at her.

While I sat by the creek I heard a strange cat-like sound to my left. Then three sleek heads emerged from the stream. The river otters had arrived and, like always, they looked like well oiled serpents. I watched as the otters periodically swam by, popping their heads out of the water every once in a while. Shortly thereafter a cow moose walked out in the creek and crossed over into the trees on the far shore. A hummingbird then flashed through camp right in front of me doing its lifelong impression of a helicopter. Then, in short order, another river otter swam by. The osprey returned to its perch at the top of a tall pine on the far side of the creek. A group of six wood ducks flew in, landed in the water, and fed before me. All of this happened in the hour that I spent contemplating and reflecting by the shores of Washington Creek.

At about 4:00 PM we packed up our gear, hoisted our packs for a final time, and walked down to Windigo. At Windigo I picked up a ceramic box decorated with otters that the store manager had put aside for me. I stopped at the visitor center to turn in my trip itinerary. There I spent some time talking to Ranger Julie, a young woman who Kyle and I have gotten to know over the years. As always, Julie was cheerful and effervescent. It is always nice to talk to people who love what they do and try to help others.

Afterward, the three of us sat on the veranda outside the visitor center. While we waited for the seaplane we shared chips & soda. I looked out at Washington Harbor with mixed emotions. This had been a great trip and one I would cherish. Still, leaving a place you love is difficult. I knew that I would make every effort to return to Isle Royale as soon as possible. I hoped to return next year with my younger son, Colin. Colin will be fourteen at that time and he has heard about Isle Royale for years. The time will hopefully come when he and I hoist our packs and head out along the Greenstone or sit by Feldtmann Lake while a bull moose shakes his antlers and turns the water into a white froth. Perhaps Colin and I will sit by Washington Creek while a moose and her calf graze past. Maybe we will sit in wonder as the sun sets at Todd Harbor allowing us to see the vibrant colors in the sky and clouds. If we are very fortunate we might hear wolves together near McCargoe Cove, Lake Ritchie, or from one of the ridge tops. All of these potential memories, and oh so many more, are waiting there on the island for us to find them.

At 5:00 the seaplane came into view and landed. We exchanged places with the incoming passengers and took off right on schedule. As we lifted off from Washington Harbor I felt tears well up in my eyes. Strangely these were not tears of sorrow. Instead, my tears were the product of the powerful emotions that Isle Royale creates within me. There, below us, cormorants and loons swam. The beautiful forests of the park stretched out beneath us. There was Feldtmann Lake where we camped in a thunderstorm and saw a bull moose. Beyond lay Siskiwit Bay and its rocky beach. The Greenstone below arched its way the length of the island. Unseen trails hiked by nameless backpackers hid away in the trees.

Time passed and Isle Royale faded into the distance and the mist of memory. Questions began to rise up in my mind. When would I return? What trails should I hike next time? Will I solo hike on the island again? What does the park look like in the fall? Can my meager writing capture even a fraction of the park's shadow let alone its substance? Why does this place draw me to it so powerfully?

Answers to these questions may or may not develop. What is important is that some lessons are learned through every wilderness experience. It is in deriving meaning from what we do, even more than the actual efforts themselves, that we shape ourselves. In looking back at this trip and its solo-hiking precursor last June, I came to believe some core values even more than I had before:

1. All life is valuable and interconnected.
2. A society that does not value wilderness risks its very soul.
3. We are brethren to other living beings, and not their masters. A wolf or moose on Isle Royale leads its life as intended. Without human interference a balance is struck. If we could apply that understanding to other environmental issues our world could be a far better place.
4. Sharing a beloved place with someone uninitiated to it is a gift for all. Hopefully the new visitor will appreciate what they see. Through such sharing we improve others and us as well.
5. Watching wildlife, feeling the cool air of a forest, or looking out over the landscape from a high ridge are experiences that touch my heart. The awesome beauty & dignity of the world bespeaks a complexity beyond imagining. Each of us is part of that complex web of life. What an honor to be a small element in something so vast and inscrutable.

6. Over time the feel of my pack on my back becomes so fulfilling. Yes, at the start of a trip my pack breaks me into the trials of the trail. But then, at some point in the hike, I merge with my pack and feel comfortable and steady. On winter days I sometimes look at my pack and recall the journeys we have shared. My pack has been a trusted home away from home.

7. When we visit a place like Isle Royale we become a part of the environment. If you enter a wilderness area as an external observer you will miss much. On the other hand, if you consider yourself as a part of the forest—doors will open. The woods that house the wolves and moose are your own temporary home as well. If you feel this sense of belonging you will behave more carefully and gain more from your trip. This subtle shift of perception from visitor to participant allows you to merge with a place more fully & observe more of it.

8. The emotion that, Isle Royale, its terrain, setting, and wildlife stir in me are a sure sign of my need to return again. For some people new conquests are always in order. For me, the beloved familiarity of this great park pulls at my spirit and calls on me to come back. So, over the coming weeks and months I will pull out my trustworthy old Isle Royale trail map & plan future excursions. I can visualize myself landing at Windigo in familiar Washington Harbor. The blue water glistens in the sunlight. The woods beckon to me in their green way. Trails will be walked. Ridges will be climbed. My body and spirit will be recharged in this national treasure remotely hidden in Lake Superior's icy embrace and known as Isle Royale.

Hiking Tips:
#100: At Trip's End, Turn in your Itinerary –
When you complete your hike it is requested that you turn
in your permit and issued itinerary at the ranger station
you leave from. There the rangers will ask you if you
made any deviations form your original plan. Be honest
and let them know what you actually did. This
information is helpful to the park staff in terms of actual
campground use, park visitation patterns, average length
of stay, and other data points. Take the time to
responsibly check out in this way and thereby help the
park staff that work so hard to make your stay enjoyable.

#101: Commit Yourself to your Trip – Backpacking
is a demanding experience. The weight of your pack can
wear you down. Following a steeply graded trail uphill can
test body, mind, and spirit. Throw in biting insects, the
vicissitudes of weather, and equipment malfunctions and
you can create a daunting challenge. However, backpacking is the primary way you can enter backcountry
areas like Isle Royale. That being the case, you need to
commit yourself to the journey. A faint heart will not get
you down a tough trail like the Minong or up a steep climb
like the one coming out of Hatchet Lake. You will need a
conditioned body and a strong spirit to complete your trip.
Therefore, commit yourself and you go a long way toward
fulfilling your goal of a safe and uplifting visit.

#102: Do Not be Afraid to Return – Isle Royale has
one of the highest visitor return rates in the nation's
national park system. People who come to this jewel of a
park once, often return. If you feel a tugging sensation
inside of yourself to return to Isle Royale, go with your
heart. This trip represented my tenth visit to Isle Royale. I
have met people who have visited this park many more

times than I have. This is a magical place that, if you are predisposed to appreciate it, will win a corner in your soul. As I write these lines my mind drifts to places I have visited on the island and things I have seen. I will return again and, perhaps, we will meet on trails or in camp. If so, may your journey be safe & secure. May the charm of this place surround you and find its way into your heart as it has with my own.

Epilogue
The ridges have been climbed,
Valleys have been seen.
The miles of trail have melted away.
The journey is done, but others follow.
Returns will be made—but that is for the future.
For now, the island of my heart fades in the distance.

Part III:Fall Tips for the End of the Season

"*There is a slumbering subterranean fire in nature which never goes out, and which no cold can chill.*"

- Thoreau -

Isle Royale remains open only approximately half the year. From early May through late October the park remains available to backpackers. Final boat trips out of the various ports cease from as early as mid-September to late October. The seaplane stops traveling out to the island in September as well. By October the weather is unpredictable and potentially dangerous.

During this year of hiking I did have the opportunity to visit Isle Royale both in mid-September as well as the last week that the boat from Grand Portage was ferrying travelers to and from the island. While narratives of those trips would be somewhat redundant what I did discover was that fall hiking on Isle Royale can be a very satisfying as well as challenging experience.

If you plan on going to Isle Royale in the fall a few factors should be kept in the forefront of your mind. Among those are the following:

1. Weather is even more unpredictable than during the spring and summer.

2. Bugs will be few and far between but frosts and storms may come at any time.
3. Animal behavior will be different as you are arriving during the moose rutting season and many animals are attempting to find as much food as possible before the numbing winter.
4. While solo hiking is still a reasonable alternative you must bear in mind that the later in the season you arrive on the island the fewer emergency resources are available in case of mishap. By late October there will be virtually no staff and almost no hikers on the island. While that can be very appealing it also opens up the possibility of disaster in case of a mishap in an isolated spot.
5. Fall colors will be striking if you arrive at the right time. The red, gold, yellow, and other hues that are set off by the fall weather and light conditions are memorable and worth seeing.
6. You will have to be doubly careful about your planning. The island's stores close in the fall and you will find no margin for error in terms of items such as food, fuel, and shelter.
7. Bring enough layers so that you can cope with the cold weather. In my October trip I encountered temperatures in the low teens. Be ready for cold and precipitation because the fall is far less forgiving than other times of year.
8. Allow for extra travel days as the weather may leave you stranded for a day or more. If a fall storm kicks up its heels, Lake Superior will grind transportation to a standstill. Be sure to allow a margin for error in terms of the timing of your trip.
9. Stick as closely to your itinerary as possible. In the fall there will be few hikers and less ranger staff to check on "missing people." Let people know

where you are going and stay with your plan or at least a reasonable approximation.

10. Be prepared for the land to seem different. The fall terrain and leaf cover will open up new vistas for you. Even if you are a veteran traveler in the park, keep your eyes open and welcome in a new experience.

What follows are some additional tips that generally relate primarily to fall

Hiking in the park. While some of them have more broad based applications they do represent thoughts that came to me during my two fall hikes. Those were memorable journeys at a time of year that left me a great deal of solitude. However, let me close this introduction by restating a safety point—hiking alone in the late fall when there are so few folks on the island is a risk. If you choose to take that risk be extra careful on the trail and use the most reasoned judgment you possess

Hiking Tips:
#103: Watch out for Birds – Bird watching can be a wonderful part of a visit to Isle Royale. Some birds like loons, Merganser ducks, ravens, and gray jays can be fairly easy to spot. Others are much more reclusive. A simple tip when bird watching is to try to attend to the tree or area from which the birdcall comes. Then, carefully watch that place for any movement. With patience, you may well get a good look, or at least a glimpse, of the bird you are hearing. Also, when in camp, try to sit quietly. Some birds like jays or winter wrens will come quite close to you if you do. Another tip is to watch for nests in spring that are often built in the shelter rafters outside of the screened in enclosure. I have spent many

hours watching song sparrows feed their young from shelters and that can be a very interesting experience.

#104: Beware of Downed Leaves – If you hike in fall you will encounter leaf-covered trails. While the downed leaves are esthetically pleasing, they can be a complicating factor for hikers. The leaves can disguise the trail and confuse you. They can also be very slippery if they are even slightly damp. Downed leaves can also mask rocks, roots, puddles, and ruts that are in the trail. So, if you are hiking in those autumnal conditions be doubly cautious in terms of checking out the ground you cover. If you become confused and lose track of the trail; stop, backtrack as you need to, and carefully look for indentations among the leaves. These depressions probably represent the trail and can help you find your way back to the correct pathway.

#105: Be Doubly Prepared for bad Fall Weather – In late spring or summer being drenched by rain for a couple days is unpleasant but generally manageable. In late fall, when temperatures can regularly drop well below freezing, such a circumstance can be dangerous. Bring adequate rain gear and cold weather clothing. Plan a reasonable itinerary with room for extra days if needed. Be prepared to change your route if weather, temperature, or other weather circumstances dictate. Do not take risks. The stakes are just too high and your margin for error is much narrower than in other, more benign seasons.

#106: Look Deeply into the Forest – The leaves are down and fall has opened new windows into the forest for your potential viewing pleasure. It is amazing how different a landscape can become without the leaf cover. En route to Feldtmann Lake in October I found myself looking at ravines, streams, and small waterfalls that I had never seen before. It was as if I was hiking in a different park. Take the time to look deeply into the forest. You may be surprised by what you see.

#107: Carry Emergency Rations – Every one should strive to reduce their pack weight as much as is reasonable. Extra weight in your pack, equals increased fatigue and wear & tear in general. However, in late fall hiking where transportation can be irregular and weather conditions are more severe, it does not hurt to have some extra food. You really do not want to be stuck without rations for two days while snow and ice pile up around you as you wait for the last boat to rescue you. In the fall the services that are available to island visitors earlier in the season have disappeared. There are no eateries, camp stores, bookshops, or even public restrooms in operation. If you do not have something you need in your pack you are out of luck. So, stick a few extra provisions in your food bag and carry them just in case.

#108: Make Use of Daylight – Unlike the summer when it never seems to get dark up in the North, fall is quite a different story. In late fall it does not get light until about 8:00 AM. Darkness comes at somewhere around 7:30 PM. Every day grows shorter and, if there is cloud cover, you can eliminate at least a half hour of daylight at either end of the day. It is cold at first light and at dusk. Therefore, be sure to plan your itinerary accordingly. If you usually get a late morning start and are often the last person out of camp, you might want to rethink your past habits. Do not be overzealous in terms of daily mileage goals. Leave room for changes in your plan. To put it simply, less light means fewer possible hiking hours. Use them wisely and take advantage of the light.

#109: Be Careful Crossing Downed Trees – In the fall trail crews are no longer at work. If a tree has fallen across the trail no one will be around with tools until next May. In late fall you will encounter a fair number of such obstacles. Take your time either climbing over them or detouring around. It makes no sense to safely cover many miles only to injure yourself while moving at a snail's pace over a deadfall. Use your hiking sticks as extra supports. Be sure of each and every foot placement. Do not trust every log to bear your weight. Do not place your foot in a position where it will be trapped if you fall. Such a move can turn a common fall into a leg or ankle breaker. Get back onto the trail as soon as you clear the obstacle. If you feel turned around—pause and get your bearings. Do not let a fallen tree become a source of injury to you. Just use common sense.

#110: Dry your Tent as Soon as Possible – Tents can get wet even if they are not rained on. In cold weather condensation caused by the meeting of warmer moist air inside the tent with colder surface will often cause droplets of moisture to form. Once the tent is jammed into its stuff sack that moisture can soak it. So, once you make camp, even if you are using a shelter and have no further intention of tenting, set up your tent and dry it out. The drying process should not take very long. If there is sunshine and even a slight breeze, a half hour or so should be enough to thoroughly dry out your tent. Also, be sure to dry your tent's stuff sack. It makes little sense to go to the trouble of drying your tent only to cram it back into a wet bag. You might ask, "Why be so particular about your tent?" Well, emergencies happen and a wet tent means wet gear. Shelters you counted on getting may all be taken. Take my word—a dry tent is better than a wet one.

#111: Make Use of Solitude for Contemplation – The world can weigh heavily upon us. Not all times in our lives are happy ones. Make use of your solitudinous times in the wilderness as opportunities to contemplate the joys that life can offer. In seeing a glorious sunset or a bird in flight, we are given a gift. But there are other gifts that we already have in our possession. If you take some time in a remote place like Isle Royale to reflect on the preexisting gifts in your own life, as well as other matters of importance, you may discover things about yourself and those you love & hate. Such contemplation in a pristine setting is a gift of untold value.

#112: Be Ready to Change your Opinion –I have traditionally disliked the three mile hike leading up to Siskiwit Bay when coming from Feldtmann Lake. Yet, in late fall, that walk became something altogether different and unexpected. Trail miles I had previously disdained acquired a fresh and pleasing aspect. Do not hold your opinions so dear that they close your eyes to new visions. What was once displeasing may become pleasing in a new light. I now understand that fall is the preferred time to make this hike. To walk those miles in summer, and definitively declare them as "bad" or "boring" tells only part of the true story and is a mistake. Be prepared to change your opinions when presented with new and revealing information. An open mind is one prepared to learn. A closed mind shuts itself off from knowledge and atrophies.

#113: Care for Wet Fall Boots – If you end a hiking day with damp or soaked boots, and are traveling in late fall, be sure to care for them before turning in for the night. Frozen boots are unpleasant. Make every effort to dry out your boots with available sun and wind. If the day is inclement at least place your wet boots in a plastic bag or under cover in your tent or shelter. In a tent your body heat should help out by keeping that confined space somewhat warm. In a shelter temperatures tend to be much lower so you must be vigilant. Remember, your boots will thaw out once you start hiking, but having wet laces that turn to metal in the cold and leaded boots is an unappealing way to start your day.

#114: Watch Out for Ice – On cold fall mornings frost and ice can make leaves, rocks, and wooden surface quite slick. Be careful of your footing with every stride until things begin to thaw out. Be particularly careful on boardwalks. These helpful structures can be quite slippery. Also, boardwalks are generally not something you want to slip off of as they are built in some of the boggiest parts of the hike. When walking on slick boardwalks take a more measured stride and do not hurry. Make determined use of your hiking sticks in order to avoid a messy fall. Remember, getting soaked in a bog when it is ninety degrees is unpleasant but something you can shake off and laugh about later. The same incident when it is below twenty degrees is no laughing matter.

#115: Try To Recognize Animals' Emotions – Of course, it is vital to know the threat behaviors animals you may encounter in the wild. You do not want to be in the position of looking at a large bull moose and wondering, "Well, let's see, he's waving his antlers back and forth while also lowering his head. He keeps looking right at me, and he's taken several small strides in my direction. I wonder if this is bad?" Learn the anxious behaviors of moose, wolves, foxes, loons, and other Northwoods residents. But also attend to the way animals and birds react to you, one another, and other species. Why can smaller birds drive off an eagle by diving at it? When moose nuzzle one another, how deep does their bond of affection go? On the mainland, why do white tail deer stamp their feet when they know they are being watched? How intelligent are otters? Why do fox kits play so much? These, and innumerable other questions about wildlife, can get you deeper in touch with the fascinating and valuable lives that our fellow creatures lead.

#116: Almost Always put your Pack Cover On – Unless it is exceedingly hot and clear, and your pack cover will impede air circulation around your back, it makes sense to put your pack cover on. Keeping your pack dry comes a close second to maintaining your own safety on the trail. Your pack is your portable home. If it gets drenched you are in trouble. So why not protect it with the waterproof pack cover you possess? By putting your pack cover on in all weather you ward off dews, damps, surprise showers, minor falls into wet areas, and a host of other potentially sodden misfortunes. By not using your pack cover you create an unnecessary vulnerability while still having to carry your unused pack cover. This seems like a no brainer but it certainly remains one of many personal preferences on the trail.

#117: Consider Who you are Leaving Behind, and Periodically Remember Them – On my October trip I found myself missing my family more than on many prior occasions. Perhaps it was the cumulative number of days I had already spent on Isle Royale that year. Maybe other factors were involved that made me more homesick than had been the norm in the past. In my loneliness, I found that by periodically thinking about my loved ones I actually felt like I was carrying them along with me on the trail. The great writer and psychiatrist Viktor Frankl once wrote a powerful account of his time in German concentration camps titled *Man's Search for Meaning*. In that moving and powerful book Dr. Frankl wrote about the fact that his memories of his beloved wife had helped him survive even the worst times he experienced in the German camps. In a less powerful, but nonetheless very sincere way, my remembrances of my family and friends helped me climb the ridges and make this journey. A person's memories of those whom they love and cherish can both deepen the value of a hike and sustain them when the trail supreme tests.

#118: Do not Expect to Surprise Animals on the Trail in Fall – Seeing wildlife on the trail is usually a bracing surprise. To come around a corner on a hike only to find a moose grazing in your path is thrilling. In late fall the heavy leaf cover on the trail makes such chance encounters much less likely. Footsteps become just too noisy to allow for many of these surprise encounters. While not impossible, it certainly becomes more improbable for a hiker to sneak up on an animal or bird. If you want to see wildlife in the fall when the leaves are down look for likely spots and take your trail breaks there. Sit quietly and you may be fortunate enough to see something. As you near camp, scope out good wildlife habitats. Go back to them once you have established camp and sit quietly for a while. Remain quiet in camp while keeping your eyes and ears open. Look deeply into the denuded forest and you may see the birds and mammals that surround you.

#119: Pay Proper Respects – The Chippewa or Ojibway people who called this land home for so many years before the coming of the Europeans had a host of spiritual rituals that involved the land and the life that encompassed their world. When a deer, moose, or other animal was killed in order to sustain their lives experienced Native American hunters would thank the animal for its sacrifice. Travelers on or near Gitchegumee, as the Native Americans called Lake Superior, would offer a gift of tobacco as a token of their respect for the mighty lake. These rituals may strike modern people as odd—or they may strike a kindred chord of meaning. Paying proper respect to a lake, trail, shelter, or stream that has served you well is an act of commemoration. By thanking anyone or anything that teaches us we behave in an honorable manner. Depending upon your beliefs, prayers or meditations can serve a similar purpose. At any rate, paying respect to a place like Isle Royale cannot hurt anyone and may well help at least one person—you.

#120: Cope with Change – Life is thoroughly unpredictable. That being said—try to cope with its inconsistencies as well as you can. Some trail days are better than expected. Others are surprisingly dismal. Nevertheless, they are all part of your unique life circle. By adjusting to chance, we befriend it and make our lives better. The alternative is to attempt to make the world always fit our own needs. That is a pathway leading to disappointment.

#121: Even when hiking Alone, Pack some Dinners for Two – If you look closely at the caloric content of many dehydrated meals for two you will discover that they do not contain that many more calories than the single meals do. On a backpacking trip you will burn a great many calories. Your daily food intake will not match your output. Over time you may well feel an energy ebb tide. Therefore, pack some dinners for two and eat them yourself. The somewhat larger portion size will give you the equivalent of a smaller second serving. In this way you can gain some needed calories while carrying only a few extra ounces in your pack. You need not be a glutton on the trail but every third or fourth day that extra serving will be appreciated.

#122: Try Vegetarian Meals – Dehydrated meals come in a wide variety of flavors. While most backpackers are probably not vegetarians, the choice of vegetarian dehydrated meals is a viable one to consider. In my own experience the vegetarian dehydrated meals are generally tastier than their meaty counterparts. In terms of calories, nutrition, and energy potential— vegetarian meals are the equal of the meat dishes. One factor on a longer trip that can be a drag is the redundancy of diet. By adding vegetarian meals to your food bag you expand the potential menu for the trip. Take my word for it—items such as pasta prima vera, three-cheese lasagna, and meatless chili will hit the spot.

#123: Prepare for a Day Hike in a Reasonable Way – For backpackers, having the opportunity to "slack pack" or day hike with a greatly lightened load, is a welcome treat. On Isle Royale there are opportunities to build day hikes into your itinerary. Places such as Windigo, McCargoe Cove, Daisy Farm, and Rock Harbor are a few examples of areas where a day hike can be part of your trip. If you plan on day hiking on Isle Royale, or elsewhere, it is important that you carry what you need with you on the trail. There is a tendency to take day hiking too lightly. Even though you are carrying a fraction of your usual pack weight you still should be careful. Accidents and injuries can happen on any hike—so be prepared. Listed below is a partial menu of items I usually carry with me when day hiking. This is hardly an immaculate list but it should give you some basis for creating your own.

Day Hiking List
1. Compass
2. Water Filter
3. Spare Socks
4. Rain Coat
5. Tarp or Emergency Shelter
6. Snacks
7. First Aid Kit
8. Toilet Paper
9. Journal & Pens
10. Spare Boot Laces
11. Headlamp
12. Candles & Matches
13. Map
14. Pack Cover
15. Two Water bottles
16. Insect Spray

#124: Bring Two Eating Utensils – If you are a clod like me you will better understand this tip. It seems that every few trips I end up stepping on, or in some way breaking my spoon. Therefore, because of my own awkwardness I always pack a spare utensil. They weigh practically nothing and, for me, come in handy. I really do not want to be in a position to have to eat every meal with my fingers, so I carry a spare utensil. If that idea makes any sense to you then try it as well.

#125: Do not let Cabin Fever get to You – When I find myself stuck in a tent or shelter due to rain it sometimes gets to me. I want to be out on the trail using my energy and seeing things. Simply put—I sometimes suffer from cabin fever. If you are prone to this malady be sure to have what some teachers call "sponge activities." Sponge activities are extra work tasks or high interest jobs that teachers can give to students who have high energy levels as well as a need for action and movement. A sponge activity is designed to "soak up" those energies and keep things stable. In camp journaling, reading, card playing, conversation, meditation, exercise, and eating can all be sponge activities. For example, when I was stuck in my shelter on this trip I found yoga to be a great relaxation activity. Think up your own sponge activities and use them to transform cabin fever into productive time.

#126: Do not let your Observation Harm Wildlife – When you see a moose cow and calf it can be a magical moment. However, your magical moment can turn into tragedy if your presence causes the cow to run off and abandon her calf. When observing wildlife try to remember this cardinal rule—if your presence is changing the animal's behavior in an obvious way, move on. There are many temptations to want to get closer and closer to animals or birds. There is nothing wrong in using stealth to allow yourself the treat of watching a wild creature without it knowing you are there. But, once your presence is known, do not let your own personal needs endanger both the creatures you are observing and you as well.

#127: Bring Extra Daily Medications – If you take any sort of daily medications be sure to pack extra doses for your trip. If factors such as weather or mishap alter your travel schedule you will at least have your required medications on hand. Also, if you become ill or are injured, you will have a ready supply of your key medications. Pills or capsules weigh next to nothing but they are an important part of a person's regimen. So, pack backup dosages and eliminate one more thing to worry about.

Do not pursue the past.
Do not lose yourself in the future.
The past no longer is.
The future has not yet come.
Looking deeply at life as it is
in the very here and now,
the practitioner dwells in stability &
freedom.

- Buddha -

Hiking Tips Index

Tip #/Topic/Page #
1 Prepare Physically & Mentally 8-9
2 Set Your Own Pace 9
3 Watch Fluid Intake 9
4 Listen More & Talk Less 9
5 Use Two Hiking Poles 9-10
6 People are part of the Landscape 10
7 Stay on Durable Surfaces 10
8 Learn How to Fall 15
9 When Crossing Boardwalks
   Pay Attention 15
10 Do Not Underestimate Trails 16
11 Do Not Rush at Day's End 16
12 Wear Quick Drying Clothes 16
13 Repackage Your Foodstuffs 17
14 Bring Toilette Paper 17
15 Do Not Just Look for One Thing 17
16 Avoid Cross Over Steps 26
17 Never Rush Stream Crossings 26
18 Do Not Collect Souvenirs 26-27
19 Follow Your Own Daily Rhythm 27
20 Bring Reading Materials 27

21 Pack as Light as is Practicable 33-34

22 Maintain a Journal 34

23 Pack Out What You Pack In 34

24 Bring Camp Shoes 34

25 Observe the Minute Life Around You 34-35

26 Pack Layers of Clothing 35

27 Think of Your Trip as a Journey
And Not a Race 35

28 The Difficult & the Easy
Complement Each Other 43

29 Let Your Wheels Move
Along Old Ruts 44

30 I Hold Firmly to Stillness 44

31 One Who Excels in Traveling
Leaves No Wheel Tracks 44

32 If You Would Take From a Thing
You Must First Give to It 44-45

33 Know When to Stop & You Will
Meet No Danger 45

34 The further One Goes the Less
One Knows 45

35 A Journey of a Thousand Miles
Begins with a Single Step 45

36 Not to Know & to Think that
You Know will lead to Difficulty 45-46

37 Think About Hydration 51

38 Bring Plenty of Moleskin 51-52
39 Cary Spare Socks & Liners 52
40 Use Gatorade or Other Enhancement 52
41 Watch for Moose at Windigo 52
42 Use the *Voyageur II* for Re-Supply 53
43 Rest at Day's End 54
44 Slow your Pace on Wet Trails 59
45 Be Careful on Wet Rocks 59-60
46 Cover Up in Camp 60
47 Hike in Shorts 60-61
48 Bring Enough Bug Spray 61
49 Try to Think Like an Animal 61
50 Watch for Cairns 70-71
51 Use Dehydrated Foods 71
52 Pack some Candles 71
53 Do Not Plan on Campfires 71-72
54 Wear Solid Footgear 72
55 Bring a Lightweight Camera 72
56 Share Helpful Advice 72-73
57 Bring a Reliable Water Filter 73
58 Be Creative with your Itinerary 73
59 If Solo Hiking be Cautious 74
60 Plan Well if Hiking with Rookies 81-82
61 If Possible Build Flextime In 82
62 Listen to the Woods 82-83
63 Always have Time for Humor 83

64 Do Not Take yourself too Seriously 83-84

65 Close Your Eyes & Pause 88

66 Share a Beloved Place with Rookies 88

67 Only Use Bug Spray When you Must 88-89

68 Break in Easy 89

69 Be Patient with Yourself & Others 89-90

70 When Hiking Downhill,
Watch your Feet 95

71 On Ascents Watch your Spacing 95-96

72 Put Rookies in the Middle
Of the Group 96

73 Take Breaks at the Top 96-97

74 In Dry Weather do not Take
Water for Granted 97

75 Readjust your Pack as Needed 97-98

76 Bring a Deck of Cards 103

77 Bring a Headlamp 102

78 Beware of Leeches 103

79 At Least Change your Socks 103-104

80 Respect Boiling Water 104-105

81 Travel with Kindred Spirits 111

82 Double-check Camp 111

83 Respect All Life 111-112

84 Bring Spare Bootlaces 112

165

85 Carry Trail Lessons Home 112-113

86 Leave No Trace 120

87 Honor Campground Rules 120-121

88 Make Camp & Then Relax 121

89 Do not See Life Through a Lens 121

90 Give Way to Uphill Hikers 121

91 Stretch 128

92 Invert Liner Socks 128

93 Appropriate Human Waste Disposal 129

94 Hike on Durable Surfaces 129

95 Know how to Repair your Filter 133

96 Know Something the Destination 133-134

97 Know First Aid Basics 134-135

98 Follow Your Itinerary 135

99 Help Others 135-136

100 Turn in your Permit 145

101 Commit to the Hike` 145

102 Do not be Afraid to Return 145-146

103 Watch for Birds 150-151

104 Beware of Downed Leaves 151

105 Doubly Prepare for Fall Weather 151

106 Look Deeply into the Fall Woods 151

107 Carry Emergency Rations 153

108 Make Use of Daylight 152

109 Be Careful Crossing Downed Trees 152-153

110 Dry Your Tent ASAP 153

111 Use Solitude for Contemplation
153-154

112 Be Ready to Change your Opinion 154

113 Care for Wet Fall Boots 154

114 Watch Out for Ice 154-155

115 Try to Recognize Animals' Emotions
155

116 Put your Pack Cover On 155-156

117 Remember Those Left Behind 156

118 In Fall Surprising Animals is Rare
156-157

119 Pay Proper Respects 157

120 Cope with Change 157-158

121 Solo Hikers can eat Dinners for Two
158

122 Try Vegetarian Meals 158

123 Plan Day Hikes Well 158-159

124 Bring Two Eating Utensils 159-160

125 Avoid Cabin Fever 160

126 Be Careful When Observing Wildlife
160

127 Bring Adequate Medication Dosages
160-161

The secret waits for the insight
Of eyes unclouded by longing;
Those who are bound by desire
See only the outward container

- Lao Tzu -

Resource Guide

I. Park Service Information: If you are interested in visiting Isle Royale you can get information from the park at http://www.nps.gov/isro/. Information, can also be received by writing:

Isle Royale National Park
800 East Lakeshore Drive
Houghton, MI 49931-1895

II. Transportation to the Park: Information about transportation can be received by using the contact information below:

Voyageur II & Wenonah (**Grand Portage, MN**):

http://www.grand-isle-royale.com/
GPIR Line, Inc.
1507 North First Street
Superior, Wisconsin 54880
715-392-2100
1-888-746-2305

Isle Royale Queen IV (**Copper Harbor, MI**):

The Isle Royale Line
Waterfront Landing
Copper Harbor, Michigan 49918

Telephone: (906) 289-4437
Fax: (906) 289-4952

NPS Ranger III (Houghton, MI)

Isle Royale National Park
800 East Lakeshore Drive
Houghton, MI 49931-1869
Phone (906) 482-0984
Fax (906) 482-8753
Email ISRO_Ranger3Reserve@nps.gov

Seaplane Service **(Hancock, MI):**

Royale Air Service, Inc.
PO Box 15184
Duluth, MN 55815
(218) 721-0405
Toll Free (877) 359-4753
FAX (877) 359-4754 & (218) 721-0409
E-mail: info@royaleairservice.com

III. Park Maps: Maps of the park can be found at:
http://www.closertonature.com/maps/isle-royale-map.htm
http://www.isle.royale.national-park.com/map.htm

IV. Isle Royale Natural History Association (IRNHA):
References, topographical maps, books, and a host of
other valuable information regarding the park can be
purchased from the Isle Royal Natural History
Association (IRNHA) at:
Isle Royale Natural History Association
800 East Lakeshore Drive
Houghton, Michigan 49931
Office hours: 8 a.m.-4:30 p.m. (EST), Monday-Friday
Call TOLL-FREE (800) 678-6925 or (906) 482-7860

irnha@irnha.org

V. Recommended Reading: While there is no specific park guidebook potential visitors should refer to:

Allen, Durward L. *Wolves of Minong: Their Vital Role in a Wild Community,* Boston, MA: Houghton Mifflin, (1979), ISBN: 0-395-27626-8

Curtis, Rebecca S. *Charlotte Avery on Isle Royale,* Mount Horab, WI: Midwest Traditions, Inc., (1995), ISBN: 1-883953-13-8

Dennis, Roy. *Loons,* Stillwater, MN: Voyageur Press, (1993), ISBN: 0-89658-224-8

Dufresne, Jim. *Isle Royale National Park: Foot Trails & Water Routes,* Seattle, WA: The Mountaineers, (1991), ISBN: 0-89886-283-3

Gostomski, Ted & Marr, Janet. *Island Life: An Isle Royale Nature Guide,* MI: IRNHA Press, (2007), ISBN: 978-0935289152

Grambo, Rebecca L. *The World of the Fox,* San Francisco, CA: Sierra Club Books, (1995), ISBN: 0-87156-958-2

Janke, Robert A. *The Wildflowers of Isle Royale,* Houghton,), ISBN: 0935289-08-9

Parratt, Smitty & Welker, Doug. *The Place Names of Isle Royale,* Houghton, MI: IRNHA Press, (1999), ISBN: 0-935289-10-0

Peterson, Carolyn. *A View from the Wolf's Eye,* Houghton, MI: IRNHA Press, (2008), ISBN: 978-0-935289-16-9

Peterson, Rolf. *The Wolves of Isle Royale: A Broken Balance,* Minocqua, WI: Willow Creek Press, (1995), ISBN: 1-57223-031-2

Rennicke, Jeff. *Isle Royale: Moods, Magic, & Mystique,* Houghton, MI: IRNHA Press, (1989), ISBN: 0-935289-01-1

Romaneck, Greg M. *A Superior Journey: Trail Reflections from Isle Royale National Park,* Bloomington, IN: AuthorHouse, (2005), ISBN: 1-42083-477-0

Silliker, Bill. *Moose: Giant of the Northern Forest,* Buffalo, NY: Firefly Books, (1998), ISBN: 1-55209-255-0

Simonson, Dorothy. *The Diary of an Isle Royale School Teacher,* Houghton, MI: IRNHA Press, (1999), ISBN: 0-935289-02-X

Skelton, Napier. *Superior Wilderness: Isle Royale National Park,* Houghton, MI: IRNHA Press, (1997), ISBN: 0-935289-09-7

Stall, Chris. *Animal Tracks of the Great Lakes,* Seattle, WA: The Mountaineers, (2000), ISBN: 0-89886-196-9

Strong, Paul. *Where Waters Run: Beavers,* Minnetonka, MN: Northwood Press, (1997), ISBN: 0-55971-580-4

VI. Web Sites: The following web sites offer some interesting information about various aspects of Isle Royale:

http://www.nyx.net/~sjhoward/Isle_Royale/
http://www.isleroyale.info/cgi-local/teemz/teemz.cgi
http://sweetwatervisions.com/Pages/isleroyale.html
http://www.intellicast.com/IcastPage/LoadPage.aspx?loc=usmipk40&seg=LocalWeather&prodgrp=Forecasts&product=Forecast&prodnav=none
http://www.isle.royale.national-park.com/
http://gorp.away.com/gorp/resource/us_national_park/mi_isle.htm
http://www.terragalleria.com/parks/np.isle-royale.all.html

VII. Rock Harbor Lodge: The lodge can be contacted for reservations, sponsored boat trips, and other matters at:

http://rockharborlodge.com/
Rock Harbor Lodge (Summer Season)
PO Box 605 - Houghton MI 49931

Rock Harbor Lodge (Winter Season)
PO Box 27 - Mammoth Cave KY 42259

VIII. Annual Ecological Study of Wolves & Moose on Isle Royale: For nearly five decades researchers have studied the numbers and welfare of the moose and wolf population on Isle Royale. On an annual basis a written report is made regarding data compiled relative to these two park species. Dr. Rolf Peterson of Michigan Technological University in Houghton, MI has spearheaded this reporting for many years. The annual report can be purchased via the NPS or IRNHA in a bound version. It can also be accessed at:
http://www.isleroyalewolf.org/

IX. Six Suggested Pack Books: Here are a handful of suggestions for books you might consider packing with you if you head out to Isle Royale or any other backpacking adventure.

1. *Walking: A little Book of Wisdom* by Henry David Thoreau: A wonderful short look at the joy of walking and the meaning of wilderness written by the great 19th century American philosopher and trekker.
2. *Peace With Every Step: The Path of Mindfulness in Everyday Life* by Thich Nhat Hanh: This beautiful look at balance in life written by a man who was once nominated for the Noble Peace Prize by Dr. Martin Luther King and remains a leading expert on Buddhist compassion is a book to be treasured.

3. *The Art of War* By Sun Tzu: This 2000-year-old classic investigates the role of thoughtfulness in overcoming obstacles and remains one of the most thought-provoking works of Taoist philosophy available.
4. *The Tao Te Ching* by Lao Tzu: This slim centerpiece of Taoism stands out as a wonderful source of everyday wisdom and reflection on the trail and in life in general.
5. *Walking With Spring* by Earl V. Shaffer: Written by the first person to successfully thru-hike the Appalachian Trail, this account offers insights into backpacking, long distance travel, pilgrimages, and people's ability to perform honorably even under the most adverse conditions.
6. *A Walk in the Woods: Rediscovering America on the Appalachian Trail* by Bill Bryson: A sometimes humorous look at a middle-aged man's attempt to thru-hike America's oldest long distance hiking trail. Readers will come away with memories of foibles on the trail, great effort, and the ability to laugh at both adversity and oneself. Most people who backpack with any regularity will find things to identify with in this fine book.

"What would human life be without forests, those natural cities?"

-Thoreau -

www.ingramcontent.com/pod-product-compliance
Lightning Source LLC
Chambersburg PA
CBHW030012110426
42741CB00032B/331